SIGNS
OF
THE
TIMES

Books by M. R. De Haan

Adventures in Faith
Bread for Each Day
Broken Things
The Chemistry of the Blood
Coming Events in Prophecy
Daniel the Prophet
The Days of Noah
Dear Doctor: I Have a Problem
508 Answers to Bible Questions
Genesis and Evolution
Studies in Hebrews
The Jew and Palestine in Prophecy
Studies in Jonah
Law or Grace
Our Daily Bread
Pentecost and After
Portraits of Christ in Genesis
Studies in Revelation
The Romance of Redemption
The Second Coming of Jesus
Signs of the Times
Simon Peter
Studies in First Corinthians
Studies in Galatians
The Tabernacle

M. R. De Haan Classic Library

SIGNS
OF
THE
TIMES

M. R. DE HAAN

B. McCALL BARBOUR
28 GEORGE IV BRIDGE
EDINBURGH EH1 1ES, SCOTLAND

kregel
PUBLICATIONS

Grand Rapids, MI 49501

Library of Congress Cataloging-in-Publication Data

De Haan, M. R. (Martin Ralph), 1891–1964.
[Signs of the times and other prophetic messages]
   Signs of the times / M. R. De Haan.
       p.   cm. (M. R. De Haan classic library)
   Originally published: Grand Rapids, Mich.: Zondervan, 1951.
    1. Eschatology—Semons. 2. End of the world—
Sermons 3. Sermons, American I. Title. II. Series: De
Haan, M. R. (Martin Ralph), 1891–1964. M. R. De Haan
classic library.
BT823.D44   1997   236'.9—dc20   96-32045
                                              CIP

ISBN 0-8254-2484-4

Printed in the United States of America
2 3 4 5 / 01 00

Dedication

To the many thousands of faithful friends of the *Radio Bible Class* who have enabled us to broadcast the Gospel of our soon-coming Saviour around the world for the past thirteen years, who, by their prayers have upheld our hands, by their letters have encouraged our hearts and by their support have helped us press ever onward, this volume is gratefully dedicated.

Contents

Introduction

The lectures in this volume were first broadcast over the world-wide radio facilities employed by the *Radio Bible Class*. The response to these messages was so enthusiastic that the need for combining these sermons in one volume was soon felt. The following chapters have been gathered from these and similar broadcasts because of the unusual blessing received by the listeners when they first heard the lectures delivered over the air.

We send this volume forth with the earnest prayer that the blessings received by our listeners may be greatly multiplied in the hearts of all who shall read them in this form.

The Lord gave the word: great was the company of those that published it (Psalm 68:11).

M. R. De Haan, M.D.

CHAPTER ONE

The Certainty of Christ's Return

> The Pharisees also with the Sadducees came, and
> tempting desired him that he would shew them a sign
> from heaven.
>
> He answered and said unto them, When it is evening,
> ye say, It will be fair weather: for the sky is red.
>
> And in the morning, It will be foul weather to day:
> for the sky is red and lowring. O ye hypocrites, ye can
> discern the face of the sky; but can ye not discern the
> signs of the times? (Matthew 16:1-3)

When the Lord Jesus Christ came into the world over nineteen hundred years ago, His coming had been so minutely foretold that we wonder how anyone could fail to recognize Him
when He came. As someone has said, "Jesus came into the
world with so many identification tags on Him that it seems
no one could miss recognizing Him as the promised Messiah
when He finally came." His coming had been foretold in
hundreds of prophecies, His ministry heralded by John the
Baptist and evidenced by all the signs which the prophets had
foretold. It seems that the theologians of that day should
immediately have recognized this One, whose coming was
the theme of all the Old Testament prophecies and Scriptures.
The prophets had foretold the tribe from which He would
come, the line of His genealogy, the place where He would
be born in Bethlehem and even prophesied His virgin birth.
Yet, when He came, they missed Him entirely.

His Miracles

In addition to all these identification marks, He came also with signs and wonders and miracles, to prove that He was the promised Messiah. He healed the sick, cleansed the lepers, raised the dead, cast out demons, walked on the water and gave a thousand other evidences that He was the One who indeed was to come. In spite of all this, they would not believe on Him. So, in this passage of Scripture, the theologians came asking for a sign from heaven. Jesus refused them entirely, castigating them severely for not being able to read the signs of the times and understand the Scriptures. They might have known, they *should* have known the Scriptures well enough to have been expecting Him at this very time. Jesus calls them hypocrites who are able to discern the face of the sky but are ignorant of the signs of the times.

Jesus Is Coming Again

This same Jesus, who came nineteen hundred years ago, is coming back again, for He is now in heaven and waiting to return. No one who takes his Bible seriously can doubt the return of the Lord Jesus Christ. His Second Coming is mentioned two hundred and forty times in the New Testament alone, more times by far than any other doctrine in the entire Bible. There is no more certain truth in the entire Scriptures than the personal, literal, imminent return of the Lord Jesus Christ to this earth.

An Undated Event

The exact day of this great event, however, has not been revealed. We know not when He will come as far as the day and the hour are concerned. All attempts to fix dates, therefore, are absolutely un-scriptural and can only bring reproach upon the cause of Christ. All the date-setters of the past have proved to be false prophets. Jesus Himself said in Matthew 24:36, "But of that day and hour knoweth no man, no not the angels of heaven, but my Father only." We, therefore, reject every attempt of men to fix the date of our Lord's return.

THE TIMES AND THE SEASONS

When we say that we cannot know the day or the hour, it does not mean that we cannot know the "times and the seasons." We are told definitely that we may know when it is near and the general time when He will come back again. One thing we do know, we are nearer the coming of Christ today than we have ever been before in all of history. Each day brings us one day closer to this certain event. The Bible abounds with signs which will reveal to the spiritual Christian the nearness of His Second Coming. To ignore these signs is to make ourselves partakers of the sin of the hypocrites of Jesus' day who were rebuked and castigated for not knowing the signs of His First Coming.

Jesus Himself gave us scores of signs and indications which He said would precede His coming again by which we might know that His coming is imminent. Again and again, in speaking of these signs, He assures us, "When ye shall see all these things, know that it is near, even at the doors" (Matthew 24:33).

There are, then, two dangers. First, the danger of date setting, and, second, the opposite evil, just as serious, of ignoring the signs of the times which tell us when Jesus is about to come again. The believer need not be ignorant concerning the time of our Lord's return. Some time ago I heard a preacher speaking on the Second Coming who said, "No one can know when Jesus is coming again, for He will come as a thief in the night. The thief does not announce his coming or give any indication of when he may be expected." This brother then quoted I Thessalonians 5, verses 2 and 3:

> For yourselves know perfectly that the day of the Lord
> so cometh as a thief in the night.

> For when they shall say, Peace and safety; then sudden destruction cometh upon them, as travail upon a woman with child; and they shall not escape.

There he stopped. Why stop there? Why not read verse 4 of I Thessalonians 5 and the verses which follow as well? Jesus comes as a thief for the unsaved, to be sure, but certainly this passage was not spoken concerning the believer. Here is the passage which follows:

> But ye, brethren, are not in darkness, that that day should overtake you as a thief.
>
> Ye are all the children of light, and the children of the day: we are not of the night, nor of darkness.
>
> Therefore let us not sleep, as do others; but let us watch and be sober (I Thessalonians 5:4-6).

Notice carefully, the coming of the Lord will *not* come as a thief for the believer at all. That applies only to the unsaved. For this reason, the true Christian studies the signs of the times as given in the Scriptures that he may know when Jesus' coming is near. To fail to acquaint ourselves with the signs of His return will merit the rebuke of the Lord Jesus Himself who said, "O ye hypocrites, ye can discern the face of the sky; but can ye not discern the signs of the times?" (Matthew 16:3)

MANY SIGNS

Space does not permit us to discuss all the signs of Jesus' return as found throughout the Scriptures. Our Lord gives a long list of signs in Matthew 24, in Luke 21 and in Mark 13. Almost without exception, the writers of the epistles, under the inspiration of the Holy Spirit, add many more to the long list. In Matthew 24 alone we find the signs of false teachers, false prophets, wars and rumors of wars, pestilences, famines, earthquakes in divers places, race hatred, anti-semitism, hatred among brethren, religious apostasy, the universal preaching of the Gospel unto all the world and the budding of the fig tree. Paul the Apostle adds a great many more when he says to Timothy,

> This know also, that in the last days perilous times shall come.
>
> For men shall be lovers of their own selves, covetous, boasters, proud, blasphemers, disobedient to parents, unthankful, unholy,
>
> Without natural affection, trucebreakers, false accusers, incontinent, fierce, despisers of those that are good,
>
> Traitors, heady, highminded, lovers of pleasures more than lovers of God;
>
> Having a form of godliness, but denying the power thereof: from such turn away (II Timothy 3:1-5).

The Apostle John adds still more. The prophets of the Old Testament, Isaiah, Ezekiel, Jeremiah, Daniel, Joel and all of the minor prophets, point out many signs of Jesus' Second Coming. Jesus said that when these things (signs) would come to pass, then His coming of a certainty would be near.

THE SCOFFERS OBJECT

I anticipate some objections to these remarks immediately. Peter foretold nineteen hundred years ago that scoffers would come in the latter days. We shall answer these critics at once. These men who deny the imminent return of Jesus tell us, "All these signs that you have mentioned—wars, pestilences, famines and earthquakes, wickedness, apostasy, antsemitism, etc., have always been here. They are nothing new. There is not a century nor a decade since these words were spoken that these things were not present upon the earth. How can they mean the coming of the Lord is near? He has not yet come. Things are no different now than they always have been." Peter told us that people would say exactly those things, for we read in II Peter,

> Knowing this first, that there shall come in the last days scoffers, walking after their own lusts,
>
> And saying, Where is the promise of his coming? for

since the fathers fell asleep, all things continue as they
were from the beginning of the creation (II Peter 3:3-4).

These scoffers, you notice, are partly right, yet tragically
wrong. It is true that in every age we have had wars, rumors
of wars, pestilences, famines, earthquakes, race hatred, violence,
false teachers and deceivers. *But,* never before in history have
they been as intense as today. There are more earthquakes recorded today than at any other time in history. This is the
word of seismologists, not the word of a preacher. There are
more rumors of wars, more false teachers, more race hatred,
more evil and immorality than ever before. The real significance lies in the fact that *all* these things are present *now* for
the first time in history at *one and the same time.*

Let me refer you to one word in the statement of Jesus in
Matthew 24:33, "So likewise ye, when ye shall see *all* these
things, know that it is near, even at the doors." The one
word I would have you notice is *all.* Jesus says when *all* these
things happen, then *know.* Today *for the first time in human
history* all the signs of the times are present, at one time. I do
not know of a single sign which needs to be fulfilled before the
Lord Jesus Christ will return.

FIVE LAST SIGNS

Within the past generation we have witnessed at least five
outstanding signs, among others, fulfillments of prophecy which
have never been present in all of history before. These five
major signs of the last days and the coming of our Lord will
occupy much of the succeeding chapters. Here are the five
amazing signs of His coming again which have never before
taken place:

1. The restoration of the nation of Israel to the land of
Palestine after twenty-five hundred years of dispersion.
2. The phenomenal rise of the king of the north, Russia,
and her allies spoken of in Ezekiel 38 and 39.

3. The formation of the United Nations, the beginning restoration of the Roman Empire for the end time.

4. The preaching of the Gospel by radio around the entire world in fulfillment of the Lord's Word that this Gospel shall be preached unto all the world.

5. The increase in knowledge and travel in the last days.

Any one of these signs by itself is already an amazing sign. Taken together with many others that we might mention, they become the most overwhelming evidence of the fact that He that "shall come will come and will not tarry." When we consider just one fact, the restoration of the nation of Israel into the land of Palestine, we have a fulfillment of hundreds and hundreds of passages of Scripture which tell us that these things would happen just before the return of the Messiah to set up His Kingdom. After twenty-five hundred years without a national existence, Israel is now in the land with her own government, her own navy, her own army, her own flag, her own constitution and her own president. She is now recognized as a member of the family of nations of the world. We will have more to say about this fact.

In the light of all the indisputable evidences, are you ready for the coming of the Lord? When He comes He will take out His own, but to the lost ones it will be the end of all opportunity and the beginning of eternal doom. Turn now and flee to the Lord Jesus Christ before it is forever too late.

CHAPTER TWO

The Importance of Christ's Return

The most certain thing in all the world is the return of the Lord Jesus Christ to this earth. The unbroken testimony of Scripture and the personal promise of our Lord Himself speaks of our Lord's return. From Genesis to Revelation the Bible is replete with the promises of His *Second Advent*. Because of the denial of the Second Coming by so many in these latter days, it is important to see from the Word of God the prominence of this truth throughout the Scriptures. There are a great many believers who are under the false impression that, while the Bible teaches the Second Coming, it is not a cardinal doctrine, not a doctrine of great importance and not necessarily fundamental. They say, "Of course, we believe in the Second Coming, but after all it is not a fundamental doctrine. It is not essential to salvation."

Such statements reveal that the ones who hold such an opinion have not studied the Word of God and have not searched the Bible carefully. If these folks are right, then the Holy Spirit certainly made a mistake by giving this truth of the return of Christ such a prominent place throughout the entire Bible. Without His Second Coming, the First Coming of Christ is incomplete, and His work is a partial failure. Without His Second Coming, hundreds of passages in the Bible are untrue, the apostles and the prophets were tragically deceived, God becomes unfaithful and Jesus Christ Himself was mistaken concerning His coming again. There can be no hope for the world, for Israel or for the believer without belief in the fact of the Second Coming of Christ for His own.

PROMINENCE OF THE EVENT

To quote all the passages in the Old and New Testament dealing with the Second Coming of Christ and the events associated with it would mean quoting about one-third of the entire Bible. About one verse in three deals with some phase of the Second Coming of the Lord Jesus Christ. The very first promise in the Bible is a promise of the Second Coming of Jesus Christ. In Genesis 3, verse 15, God declares war on the devil in these words, "And I will put enmity between thee and the woman, and between thy seed and her seed; it shall bruise thy head, and thou shalt bruise his heel."

There are two promises contained in this verse, one concerning the First Coming, the other promise concerning the Second. The promise of the First Coming is the bruising of the heel of the seed of the woman, who is Jesus Christ. This promise was literally fulfilled nineteen hundred years ago when the Lord Jesus was nailed to the Cross of Calvary and His heel bruised against the cruel Cross. There is another promise in this verse, however, one not yet fulfilled, the bruising of the serpent's head. This will be fulfilled at the Second Coming of Christ, according to the twentieth chapter of Revelation. Just as the first promise in the Old Testament contains the assurance of His Second Coming, so the last promise in the Old Testament also speaks of the Lord's Second Coming. In Malachi 4 the prophet is speaking of Christ's return at the Day of the Lord when he says,

> For, behold, the day cometh, that shall burn as an oven; and all the proud, yea, and all that do wickedly, shall be stubble: and the day that cometh shall burn them up, saith the Lord of hosts, that it shall leave them neither root nor branch.
> But unto you that fear my name shall the Sun of

righteousness arise with healing in his wings (Malachi 4:1-2).

You will notice that this is a promise concerning the Second Coming of the Lord Jesus Christ, here called the "Sun of righteousness." When He comes for the church in the Rapture He comes as the "Morning Star." When He comes to earth the second time, He comes as the "Sun of righteousness." The first promise, and the last promise, in the Old Testament concern our Lord's Second Coming. Between these two are hundreds of other promises by Moses, David, Job, Isaiah, Jeremiah, Ezekiel, Daniel and the rest of the prophets.

The Same in the New Testament

The same is true of the New Testament Scriptures. The first promise of the New Testament, coupled with the announcement of His First Coming, is the promise of His Second Coming. Many have missed this. In Luke, chapter 1, verse 30, the angel gives Mary the promise of our Lord's Second Coming:

> And the angel said unto her, Fear not, Mary: for thou hast found favour with God.
>
> And, behold, thou shalt conceive in thy womb, and bring forth a son, and shalt call his name JESUS.
>
> He shall be great, and shall be called the Son of the Highest: and the Lord God shall give unto him the throne of his father David:
>
> And he shall reign over the house of Jacob for ever; and of his kingdom there shall be no end (Luke 1:30-33).

This announcement of His birth is accompanied by the prophecy of His Second Coming as King to reign over the house of Jacob forever, and to establish His Kingdom. Just as the first promise in the New Testament contains the promise of His coming again, so, too, with the last promise in the New Testament and in the Bible. In Revelation 22:20 Jesus, speaking through John the Apostle, says "He which testifieth these things saith, Surely I come quickly. Amen." That is the last promise of the Holy Spirit in the Bible. Here, too, is the last prayer which is found in the Bible: "Even so, come, Lord Jesus" (Revelation 22:20).

The last promise of the Bible and the prayer with which it closes concern His coming again. How can anyone, therefore, say that the Bible does not teach the return of Jesus when the Holy Spirit places such importance and emphasis on the subject? How dare anyone say that it is not a cardinal, important, fundamental, basic doctrine? How can any one accuse us of preaching too much and too often on the truth of Christ's return? How can we avoid the truth when it is found on almost every page of the Scriptures?

THE LAST WORDS OF OUR LORD JESUS

What was the thing the Lord Jesus talked about during the last few days with His disciples? We might expect in those last few hours of His life that He would talk about the Cross and His agony and His suffering and His death. We might expect Him to look for sympathy and for pity from His followers and disciples. How surprising, then, to find that, in the last days before Calvary, He did little more than mention His coming passion, suffering and death. He talked, instead, almost exclusively and continuously about His coming again at the end of the age, and the signs of His coming again. Read carefully Matthew 24 and 25, Luke 21, Mark 11, 12 and 13 or John 14. These chapters deal with His coming again and the signs of the end of the age. In them, Jesus answers the question of His disciples, "Tell us, when shall these things be and what shall be the sign of thy coming and the end of the age?"

THE FIRST WORD FROM HEAVEN

To show further the prominence and importance in which Jesus held the truth of His return, let us examine the first message which He sent back from heaven after He had as-

cended to the Father. The disciples were with the Lord on
Mount Olivet after He had commissioned them. Then,

> . . . while they beheld, He was taken up; and a cloud
> received Him out of their sight.
>
> And while they looked stedfastly toward heaven as he
> went up, behold, two men stood by them in white apparel
> (Acts 1:9-10).

Jesus had hardly disappeared into heaven before He sent
back a message by these two men. We might imagine many
things that He would send back to comfort these disciples,
but He sent back just one message, *I am coming back again.*
Here is the message:

> . . . Ye men of Galilee, why stand ye gazing up into
> heaven? this same Jesus, which is taken up from you into
> heaven, shall so come in like manner as ye have seen him
> go into heaven (Acts 1:11).

We could go on indefinitely showing how important and
prominent this truth of Christ's return is throughout the entire
Bible. The first two books of the canon of the New Testament,
I and II Thessalonians, deal almost entirely with the Lord's
return. The importance of this doctrine of the return of the
Lord Jesus is plain to see. How much are we thinking of
and believing this wonderful truth? How often do preachers
talk about this important truth which is so prominent throughout the Scriptures? By neglecting to preach often on the
Lord's return, we are withholding from God's people those
things which they need most and which are of the greatest
comfort in these last awful days.

His Coming Near

There is only one hope for this old world today. It is "that
blessed hope" of the return of the Lord Jesus Christ for His
Church. It is also Israel's only hope, and the hope of all
the groaning creation. Man seems to have reached his last
extremity. He knows not which way to turn in his confusion
and dilemma. If men would only look up to the place where

our only hope lies, what a difference it would make in their entire outlook upon world conditions today!

Here is a secret which is precious to me. A man recently asked me, "When do you really think the Lord will come back again?"

My answer was this, "I am looking for the return of Jesus this year!"

The man looked at me in astonishment and asked, "Isn't it dangerous to say that? Suppose He doesn't come this year? Then what are you going to do?"

I answered him, "I repeat, I am looking for the return of Jesus this year. If He doesn't return this year, I shall just as eagerly be looking for Him next year." That is the attitude of the true believer—looking for His imminent return.

Jesus may come at any moment. Nothing more needs to happen as far as we can find in the Scriptures. The real question is, are you ready for that day? After all, the coming of the Lord is more than cold dogma. It is more than just something to grasp for when we are in trouble and difficulty. The coming of the Lord means the release of every believer from the curse and bondage of mortality here below, to rise to meet Him in the air and, in glorified, resurrected, renewed bodies, to serve Him forever and forever in glory.

At this time, we are, however, more particularly interested in the effect of the Second Coming of the Lord Jesus Christ upon those still unsaved and without salvation through faith in the Lord Jesus Christ. Those who have wilfully rejected the Lord Jesus and His offer of salvation during this age of grace will have no other opportunity after the Lord has returned for His Church. The Bible states clearly that "now is the accepted time; now is the day of salvation . . ." (II Corinthians 6:2). Many ask, "Who will be saved after the Church is raptured and gone?" The Bible states definitely and clearly that there will be a multitude without number of every people, tribe and nation, who will be saved after the rapture of the Church. They will be only those who have never had the opportunity of receiving the Lord Jesus Christ, however, and have never wilfully rejected His offer. These will have the gospel preached to them during the Tribulation period. The Bible says with equal clearness that those who have heard the Gospel, have heard the invitation and have wilfully rejected it, will have no opportunity after the Lord shall come. The door will be immediately shut and the Bible says that God Himself will "send them strong delusion, that they should believe a lie; that they all might be damned who believed not the truth, but had pleasure in unrighteousness" (II Thessalonians 2:11). How tremendously important it is, therefore, to make a decision immediately. The very fact that you have read this message sweeps away every excuse that you will have to offer at that time. You do have the opportunity right now. You may never have it again. Turn to Him now, before it is forever too late, and "if thou shalt . . . believe in thine heart that God hath raised him from the dead thou shalt be saved" (Romans 10:9).

CHAPTER THREE

The Sign of the Jew

The Bible, the Word of God, contains hundreds of passages dealing with the end of this present age in which we are living, and the sure return of the Lord Jesus Christ to this earth to set up His Kingdom. Many of these are familiar to Christians. We have already mentioned five signs of the Second Coming which are so clear, so definite, so unmistakable, that we wish to devote considerable time to them. The first of these five signs was the phenomenal political restoration of the nation of Israel.

RESTORATION OF ISRAEL IN PALESTINE

First and foremost among the signs of the Lord's return is the miraculous restoration of the Israelite nation in the ancient land of Palestine after twenty-five hundred years of dispersion among the nations without a national existence. True, a remnant did return about 500 B.C. under Zerubbabel, Ezra and Nehemiah. However, Israel has never been an independent nation since the days of their captivity. For twenty-five hundred years the great majority of Israel, and for the past nineteen hundred years almost all of Israel, has been scattered to the four corners of the world among every nation on the face of the earth. The Israelites have been hated and persecuted, maligned and oppressed. Attempts at their complete extermination were tried over and over and over again, from the days of Haman to the present time. In spite of all these efforts, they have never perished. They were not lost among the nations, but retained their identity as a people, imperishable and eternal as the promises of God. Now, within the past three years, this people, scattered among the Gentiles, has been suddenly reborn and established in their ancient homeland as an independent nation among the nations, recognized by the world and the family of nations, having their own land, their own flag, their own government, their own army and navy, their own constitution and their own currency. For thousands of years men said, "God is all through with Israel, the Jews will never return as a nation again to the land of Palestine." All of them have now been proved wrong, because God only can be right. All this had already been foretold centuries and millenniums before by the prophets of the Old Testament. We shall refer to only a few of these many prophecies. They should prove to be a stimulus for further study of this intriguing subject.

Their Dispersion

First, then, let us examine just a few of the hundreds of prophecies dealing with the dispersion and scattering of Israel among the nations, prophecies made long before the Israelites had entered the land of Palestine. Way back in the days of their great law-giver, Moses, before Israel had even seen the Promised land, Moses under inspiration had already said this concerning the nation of Israel,

> And I will bring the land into desolation: and your enemies which dwell therein shall be astonished at it.
> And I will scatter you (Israel) among the nations, and will draw out a sword after you: and your land shall be desolate, and your cities waste
> And ye shall perish among the nations, and the land of your enemies shall eat you up.
> And they that are left of you shall pine away in their iniquity in your enemies' lands . . . (Leviticus 26:32-33; 38-39).

Israel's history for the past centuries and the desolation of

Palestine stands as irrefutable proof of the accuracy of these words of Almighty God given by His servant, Moses. Again in Deuteronomy 28:63 and 64, Moses says,

> And it shall come to pass, that as the Lord rejoiced over you to do you good, and to multiply you; so the Lord will rejoice over you to destroy you, and to bring you to nought; and ye shall be plucked from off the land (Palestine) whither thou goest to possess it.
>
> And the Lord shall scatter thee among all people, from the one end of the earth even unto the other . . .

Could a more accurate prophecy and description than this have been given of the future of Israel? Remember that it was written thirty-five hundred years ago, before Israel had even seen the land from which God said they would be scattered.

More Details

In Deuteronomy 28 Moses continues with this prediction of Israel's dispersion:

> And among these nations shalt thou find no ease, neither shall the sole of thy foot have rest: but the Lord shall give thee there a trembling heart, and failing of eyes, and sorrow of mind:
>
> And thy life shall hang in doubt before thee; and thou shalt fear day and night, and shalt have none assurance of thy life" (Deuteronomy 28:65-66).

We have but to read the history of these persecuted sons of Jacob. Ask anyone today of the thousands of "displaced persons" of the last war to see how accurately Moses described Israel's scattering and their suffering among the nations in clear and unmistakable detail.

There are many other prophecies along this same line. Read Leviticus 26 and Deuteronomy 28, 29 and 30 to see how, to the very smallest and minutest detail, Israel's sufferings were foretold by God and their scattering among the nations was prophesied. Every one of these prophecies has been literally fulfilled. A literal people were literally scattered among literal nations and suffered literal persecution. Every living son of Jacob is a testimony to the truth of the Word of God.

THEIR RESTORATION

Now we come to the second aspect of these prophecies. Even as Israel's literal dispersion and scattering was foretold, so by these same prophets it was also foretold that they would just as literally be preserved from extinction or assimilation, and would, in the end time, just before the return of Jesus their Messiah, be brought back again as a nation into their own land of Canaan and Palestine. We could spend hours just quoting passages from the Bible, the Word of God, to prove this. Here are just a few as examples.

SAME AUTHOR

The same author who predicted Israel's scattering, so literally fulfilled, also predicted her return to the promised land. The same chapters tell of their scattering (Leviticus 26):

> And yet for all that, when they (Israel) be in the land of their enemies, I will not cast them away, neither will I abhor them, to destroy them utterly, and to break my covenant with them: for I am the Lord their God.

> But I will for their sakes remember the covenant of their ancestors, whom I brought forth out of the land of Egypt in the sight of the nations, that I might be their God: I am the Lord (Leviticus 26:44-45)

> And it shall come to pass, when all these things are come upon thee, the blessing and the curse, which I have set before thee, and thou shalt call them to mind among all the nations, whither the Lord thy God hath driven thee,

> And shalt return unto the Lord thy God, and shalt obey his voice according to all that I command thee this day, thou and thy children, with all thine heart, and with all thy soul;

> That then the Lord thy God will turn thy captivity, and have compassion upon thee, and will return and gather thee from all the nations, whither the Lord thy God hath scattered thee.

> If any of thine be driven out unto the outmost parts of heaven, from thence will the Lord thy God gather thee, and from thence will he fetch thee:
>
> And the Lord thy God will bring thee into the land which thy fathers possessed, and thou shalt possess it; and he will do thee good, and multiply thee above thy fathers (Deuteronomy 30:1-5).

Could anything be clearer and more easily understood? God said three millenniums ago what He would do in the end time. We have seen it fulfilled, in part at least, within the past two or three years.

THE OTHER PROPHETS

To these prophecies we can add the testimony of all the other prophets who agree with one accord with these words of Moses. Isaiah says in Isaiah 11:11,

> And it shall come to pass in that day, that the Lord shall set his hand again the second time to recover the remnant of His people, which shall be left, from Assyria, and from Egypt, and from Pathros, and from Cush, and from Elam, and from Shinar, and from Hamath, and from the islands of the sea.

Jeremiah the prophet adds his testimony in these words,

> And I will cause the captivity of Judah and the captivity of Israel to return, and will build them, as at the first (Jeremiah 33:7). Ezekiel the prophet also foretells the regathering of Israel when he says, For I will take you (Israel) from among the nations, and gather you out of all countries, and will bring you into your own land (Ezekiel 36:24).

Ezekiel goes on to say in the very next chapter, ". . . Behold, I will take the children of Israel from among the nations whither they be gone, and will gather them on every side, and bring them into their own land" (Ezekiel 37:21).

Here is what Amos the prophet has to say along this same line:

> And I will plant them (Israel) upon their own land, and they shall no more be pulled up out of their land which I have given them, saith the Lord thy God (Amos 9:15).

We might go on and on indefinitely and quote Daniel, Joel, Obadiah, Zephaniah, Haggai, Zechariah and Malachi. How is it possible that the great mass of Christendom should fail to see all of this with an open Bible before them? How could they fail to see this wonderful prediction of Israel's literal restoration? Those who have been preaching this literal restoration of the nation of Israel were discounted and ignored, while the teaching that the Church now is spiritual Israel and that God is all through with the Jews as a nation and with Israel was taught and believed by the masses. Thank God, we have lived to see these prophecies fulfilled and our own words verified. Our own teaching has been vindicated; our own ministry has been approved by the things which have happened. The spiritualizers of these prophecies have been silenced once and forever. Israel *is* back in the land. God *has* kept His Word literally. Those of us who have preached for years, "The Jews are going back as a nation to Palestine," were absolutely right. It always pays to believe what God says and to stick to it, no matter how impossible it may seem.

PAUL'S TESTIMONY

Already in the days of Paul the error was being taught that God was now all through with Israel, since the Day of Pentecost when the Church had been born. These teachers taught that the Church now became spiritual Israel and had now taken the place of the nation of Israel. Paul answers this question in Romans 11, when he says,

I say then, Hath God cast away his people? God forbid . . .

God hath not cast away his people which he foreknew . . .

For I would not, brethren, that you should be ignorant of this mystery, lest ye should be wise in your own conceits; that blindness in part is happened to Israel, until the fulness of the Gentiles be come in.

And so all Israel shall be saved: as it is written, There

shall come out of Zion the Deliverer, and shall turn away
ungodliness from Jacob (Romans 11:1-2; 25-26).

Now, in our own generation, during these past few years,
all of this has begun to take place. The Scriptures tell us that
when that happens the coming of the Lord is very near. If
there were no other sign of the last days, this alone would be
sufficient. Jesus Christ is coming again. When He comes you
will be judged according to this same word.

CHAPTER FOUR

The Northern Invasion

Jesus Christ is coming back to this earth again. His First coming is entirely incomplete without His Second Coming. When He came the first time He was announced as the Prince of Peace. The prophets sang of the day when the Messiah should reign, when peace would cover the entire earth, when the nations would beat their swords into plowshares and their spears into pruning hooks, when nation should rise up against nation no more, neither would they learn war at all any more. Those prophecies, made millenniums ago, have never yet been fulfilled in all of human history. When the Lord Jesus Christ was born in Bethlehem the angels chanted, "Peace on earth, good will toward men." That promise has never been fulfilled in its entirety. Right now, moreover, peace seems to be farther away from the inhabitants of the earth than ever before in all of human history.

It is all well and good to say that peace was fulfilled in the hearts of those who have received Him as their personal Saviour, but that does not exhaust the meaning of the words, "Peace on earth." The angels did not say, "Peace in the hearts of men on earth." The promise of the Word is peace, not only in the hearts of men, but among men, among nations, even among the animal creation, when "the wolf shall dwell with the lamb, and the leopard shall lie down with the kid and the young lion and the fatling together, and a little child shall lead them." The fulfillment of that prophecy lies in the future. When the Prince of Peace came the first time, man rejected Him and knew Him not. "He came into the world and the worlds were made by Him, and the world knew him not. He came unto His own and His own received Him not." The Prince of Peace was rejected. There has been no peace upon this earth since, except in the hearts of believers. The Lord Jesus Christ Himself said, "Think not that I am come to send peace on earth: I came not to send peace, but a sword" (Matthew 10:34).

Until the Prince of Peace comes back again there will never be and can never be universal peace. Man may dream of it all he wishes, but the Bible is very explicit on this matter. Every effort, honest and sincere as it may be, to bring peace without *Him*, the Prince of Peace—peace by war, peace by conference, peace by disarmament proposals, peace by appeasement, peace by force—can never succeed, for all the efforts of men must finally fail until they acknowledge Him, when He comes, who alone is the Prince of Peace.

The Situation Today

Today, this very dream of peace seems farther away than ever before, even though men are yearning for it more than they ever have. Yet the child of God and the student of the Scripture sees in all this the unmistakable proof of the truth of the Word of God and the imminent return of the Lord Jesus Christ. All these things have been prophesied and they *must* come to pass. "When they do," said Jesus, "then know that I am about to come, and the time is at hand."

All these events are signs of the time of Christ's return. There are hundreds of signs of His coming—strange sights in the heavens, meteors, smoke palls, strange objects speeding through the sky, freakish storms, the sea and the waves roaring, earthquakes, unprecedented wickedness and violence, moral decay, religious apostasy, wars and rumors of wars. All of these and many more are sure, unmistakable signs of the close of the age and the return of the Lord Jesus Christ. In former chapters, we gave what we believe to be the five most out-standing signs given in the Scriptures indicating the return of the Lord Jesus Christ. They were:

1. The phenomenal restoration of the nation of Israel
2. The phenomenal rise of the northern kingdom of Russia
3. The phenomenal formation of the United Nations
4. The phenomenal spread of the Gospel by means of radio in these last days
5. The phenomenal increase in travel and education in this last generation

The first of these, the phenomenal restoration of the nation of Israel in the land of Palestine, has already been discussed.

THE RISE OF RUSSIA

The second unmistakable prophecy of the end time is the sudden phenomenal rise of the northern kingdom of Red Russia. The Bible has a great deal to say about a power which will develop in the north in the latter days. Before quoting some of these passages from the Scripture, let me remind you that "north" in the Bible always means north of the land of Palestine. In Scripture, Palestine is the center of the surface of this earth. The very word, "Mediterranean," which bounds Palestine, means "middle of the earth." Israel's traditional enemies came down from the north again and again, and, therefore, point to the land north of the land of Palestine. In the past history of Israel it was the hosts of Assyria which were sent upon Israel by Jehovah God Himself. We are told that in the latter days another great northern power, of which Assyria was only a type, will once more sweep down upon the land of Israel and seek to destroy the nation of the Lord.

SOME SCRIPTURES

This northern power is called Gog and Magog in the Bible. It is mentioned over and over again in the Word of

God. In Ezekiel 38:15 we read of this invading army of the latter days:

> And thou shalt come from thy place out of the north parts, thou, and many people with thee, all of them riding upon horses, a great company, and a mighty army:
> And thou shalt come up against my people of Israel, as a cloud to cover the land; it shall be in the latter days (Ezekiel 38:15-16)

Again, in Ezekiel 39, we have this statement made by the prophet, "And I will turn thee back, and leave but the sixth part of thee, and will cause thee to come up from the north parts, and will bring thee upon the mountains of Israel" (Ezekiel 39:2).

Joel the prophet, in speaking of that great invading army which will come against Israel in the latter days, identifies it once again when he promises, according to the Spirit of God.

> But I will remove far off from you the northern army, and will drive him into a land barren and desolate, with his face toward the east sea, and his hinder part toward the utmost sea (Joel 2:20).

IN THE DAY OF THE LORD

This great battle by Russia against Israel is placed by Ezekiel in the latter days and by Joel in the "Day of the Lord," the Tribulation period to come.

The present phenomenal rise of this king of the north, Russia, begins to mean something in the light of prophecy as we see it unfolding before our eyes today. It is the very beginning of the end. Today, Russia's shadow has plunged all the world in deepest darkness as she raises her head, the most formidable foe of the nations in all of history. This becomes one of the most definite signs of the end of the age and of the coming of the Lord Jesus Christ.

THE THIRD GREAT SIGN

We have so far seen the fulfillment of prophecy in the restoration of the nation of Israel to the land of Palestine and the rise of Israel's enemy, Russia. We come now to the third phenomenal sign, the formation of the United Nations as we know it today. For centuries fundamental Bible teachers have pointed out that the Bible predicts the restoration of a great western alliance patterned after the ancient Roman Empire of history. It is described in great detail in Daniel's prophecy. According to the Word of God, this alliance will include the Mediterranean countries, part of Germany, France, Spain, Greece, Egypt, Britain and her colonies. Suddenly it has become a reality. While the United Nations has not yet succeeded in its original purpose to unite all the nations and to bring peace, it is nevertheless the forerunner, we are convinced, of the western confederacy of the Day of the Lord. The United Nations simply cannot succeed in bringing all nations together because God's Word said that Russia, the king of the north, and her allies, will not in the latter days be of this western alliance. The Bible describes a two-world system rather than a united world. This western alliance will be opposed to Russia and will become God's instrument in defeating Gog and Magog when she comes against Israel's land in the Tribulation period.

WHEN WILL RUSSIA STRIKE?

Remember that the western alliance of the end time, while possibly built upon the foundations laid down by the present United Nations, will, never-the-less, be quite different. It seems clear from Ezekiel 38 and 39 that Russia will strike her final blow in Palestine *after* the superman, the man of sin and the son of perdition, has risen to head the restored western empire and the federation of nations of that day. This seems clear from Ezekiel 38, verse 11. Notice the time when Russia invades Israel's land,

> And thou shalt say, I will go up to the land of unwalled villages; I will go to them that are at rest, that dwell safely, all of them dwelling without walls, and having neither bars nor gates (Ezekiel 38:11).

A careful study of the context shows that this verse refers to the nation of Israel in the land of Palestine. When Russia strikes, therefore, Israel will be at rest, dwelling safely, as they suppose, without defenses. Is this true today? Positively not. Israel is not at rest today, neither does she dwell safely. She is in constant fear of attack. At the time when Russia strikes, however, says Ezekiel, they will be at rest.

All of this is clear in the light of prophecy. After the Church has been raptured, the man of sin, the antichrist the superman, will take over the federated nations. He will lead the restored, reorganized western federation of nations, the restored Roman Empire; he will befriend Israel and bring in a false, spurious peace, a mock millennium. The temple in Jerusalem will be rebuilt under his reign, the worship of the Old Testament economy will be restored and Israel will be at rest, under the protectorate of the superman, the ruler of that day, the antichrist and the false christ.

It is then that the king of the north will strike, only to be defeated by the alliance of nations under this antichrist. Russia will be reduced to one-sixth of her original number and driven back to the wastes of Siberia. What will later happen to the armies of the antichrist after he reveals his own real character is another story. He himself will then be destroyed by God in the battle of Armageddon.

Now the pattern becomes clear. The king of the north will attack Palestine only after Israel is apparently safe and at rest under the protection of the federated western nations, led by the superman, the antichrist. According to II Thessalonians, chapter 2, this superman will not be revealed until after the Church, the body of Christ, indwelt by the Holy Spirit, has been taken out of the way. With the stage so clearly set, how near must be the coming of the Lord!

We *do not* know when our Lord may come. God is never in a hurry. We *do* know that all these signs, the restoration of Israel, the rise of Russia, the revival of the western alliance, have been prophesied as coming in the end of the age just before the return of our Lord Jesus Christ. These signs are unmistakable. Many details may remain obscure for the present and we shall not pry into them. We *do* believe His Word which says,

> And when these things begin to come to pass, then look up, and lift up your heads; for your redemption draweth nigh (Luke 21:28).
>
> So likewise ye, when ye shall see all these things know that it is near, even at the doors (Matthew 24:33).

Are you ready for that day? Any moment now the Lord may return. If you are not ready on that day, it will be forever too late.

CHAPTER FIVE

Travel and Education Signs

> But of the times and the seasons, brethren, ye have no need that I write unto you.
>
> For yourselves know perfectly that the day of the Lord so cometh as a thief in the night.
>
> For when they shall say, Peace and safety; then sudden destruction cometh upon them, as travail upon a woman with child; and they shall not escape.
>
> But ye, brethren, are not in darkness, that that day should overtake you as a thief.
>
> Ye are all the children of light, and the children of the day: we are not of the night, nor of darkness.
>
> Therefore let us not sleep, as do others; but let us watch and be sober (I Thessalonians 5:1-6).

The born-again believer in the Lord Jesus Christ should be an enlightened Christian, abreast of the times, fully aware of the program of God being carried out today. The Bible describes this program concerning the course of this age in clarity and detail. To be in darkness concerning the signs of the times and the significance of the current events which are taking place about us, to be ignorant of the nearness of Christ's return, is the result of willful ignorance and neglect of the study of the Word of God.

WE MAY KNOW THE TIME

While we cannot set the date or day of Christ's return, we may indeed know the times and the seasons of His coming again. Paul takes this for granted when he says, "But of the times and the seasons, brethren, ye have no need that I write unto you" (I Thessalonians 5:1).

Never before in the history of the Church have there been so many unmistakable, definite signs pointing to the time of Christ's return. Just to enumerate them would fill a book. Therefore, we must be content with a discussion of just a few of the more outstanding and more important signs which have recently been fulfilled. We have already studied the sign of Israel's return to Palestine, the sign of the phenomenal rise of Russia, the king of the north, and the sign of the revival of the Roman Empire and the organization of the United Nations. Next, we shall discuss the sign of the world-wide preaching of the Gospel as foretold and prophesied by the Lord Jesus. In Matthew 24 the disciples asked our Lord, "...

> . . . Tell us, when shall these things be? and what shall
> be the sign of thy coming, and of the end of the world?
> (Matthew 24:3).

In answer to this question Jesus gave a long list of signs in verses 2 to 14 of Matthew 24. He ends with this last sign in the 14th verse, "And this gospel of the kingdom shall be preached in all the world for a witness unto all nations; and then shall the end come" (Matthew 24:14).

I realize that the complete fulfillment of this prophecy will be reached in the tribulation period with the universal preaching of the Gospel of the kingdom by the hundred and forty-four thousand from the twelve tribes of Israel. By application, however, it is true today, in this present dispensation of the preaching of the Gospel of the grace of God. Some may have overlooked this remarkably significant sign which has come to pass within this generation in which we are now living.

Do you realize that within the past few years it has become possible, for the first time in history, to fulfill literally this prediction of Jesus by means of the radio? Today, for the first time in history, the Gospel of grace has reached all the world. Because of the radio there is not a square foot of the earth's surface where the message cannot be heard. From pole to pole the Gospel is being sent forth by the many faithful broadcasters throughout the world.

ALL CAN HEAR

If all the people in the world owned radios and could understand, every human being could hear this message of the Word of God. The message is carried today around the entire world. All these developments have taken place in the last twenty-five years. This, to be sure, is amazing. If there were no other sign, it would be sufficient. Added to all the rest of the signs, it becomes indisputable proof of the nearness of the coming of the Lord. I am personally convinced that the radio is God's end-time provision for the fulfillment of this last sign which Jesus gave to His disciples. It is the last opportunity for the Church to fulfill her commission, "Go ye into all the world, and preach the gospel to every creature" (Mark 16:15). It is significant that Jesus said, "And this gospel of the kingdom shall be preached in all the world for a witness unto all nations; *and then shall the end come*" (Matthew 24:14).

That last phrase "And then shall the end come," is particularly important. "When this Gospel goes throughout the world, then shall the end come." That, in effect, is what the Lord Jesus Christ is saying. That time has almost arrived. The Gospel is now circling the globe. Not once or twice, but several times, the message of salvation has circled the entire earth. In the light of these words of the Lord Jesus Christ, I declare without fear of contradiction that the coming of the Lord must be near, for He said, "Then shall the end come."

RADIO BROADCASTING

Radio gospel broadcasting is not only the quickest way to reach all men, but also the most economical, conservative way of reaching the masses. Conservative estimators tell us that for every dollar spent for broadcasting we reach over one thousand people with the message of the Gospel. That means that ten people hear this broadcast for every penny spent to put it on the air. A whole half hour of Gospel for ten people for the cost of one single penny, 1,000 people for $1.00. A hundred thousand souls hear the Gospel for a $100.00 investment while one million can be reached for the outlay of only $1,000.00. $10.000.00 will reach ten million people with the Gospel for thirty minutes. There is no other means known to man for reaching so many, so quickly, for so little. It is the fulfillment of the words of the Lord Jesus Christ, "And this gospel of the kingdom shall be preached in all the world for a witness unto all nations; *and then shall the end come"* (Matthew 24:14). He is coming again soon.

TRAVEL AND EDUCATION

Before we conclude this chapter we must call your attention briefly to a few additional signs. Two of these are found in Daniel 12, verse 4,

> But thou, O Daniel, shut up the words, and seal the book, even to the time of the end: many shall run to and fro, and knowledge shall be increased (Daniel 12:4).

Daniel, here, is speaking of the end time. In verse one of this same chapter he tells us that it will be in the Tribulation period when

> . . . there shall be a time of trouble, such as never was since there was a nation even to that same time: and at that time thy people (Israel) shall be delivered . . . (Daniel 12:1).

Notice the setting. You recognize immediately that this is the Tribulation period during which Israel shall be supernaturally delivered by her Lord. This terrible day of trouble will end at the coming of the Lord Jesus Christ to this earth. Daniel is told to shut up the words of prophecy and seal the book until the time of the end. Many of the things in prophecy will, therefore, remain sealed and unknown. At the time of the end, however, they will be revealed to the sons of men.

Then Daniel gives two of the signs of the end and the time of Christ's return. The signs are that (1) "many shall run to and fro," and (2) "knowledge shall be increased."

I call these two signs the "travel sign" and the "education sign." The time of the end will be characterized by an uprecedented increase in travel, and hitherto "undreamed-of" progress in education, knowledge, discovery and science.

THE TRAVEL SIGN

Daniel says, "Many shall run to and fro." It will be an age of unprecedented travel. It is startling to read such words written twenty-five hundred years ago by the prophet, yet so completely describing our present age. It is indeed the age of speed and travel. The world has shrunk in size many times in one generation. First came steam, then electricity; first came the train, then the diesels, the automobile, fast ships, the airplane and, now, jet planes.

Only a few years ago travel was limited. Transportation was mostly by horse and buggy, ox-teams and on foot. When I began practicing medicine less than forty years ago, I made my calls with horse and buggy, or with a cutter in the winter. There was not a mile of paved highway in the entire county. Automobiles were still a novelty. Airplanes were unknown. Few people traveled more than a few miles from their own homes. Then began the travel age, and many began to run to and fro. Today, people travel almost anywhere at will. Trains travel at almost a hundred miles an hour, autos even faster. Fast ships cross the Atlantic in a few days; planes make the trip to Europe in a few hours. The world can be circled in a few days. Our highways are jammed, airplane reservations are sold out, men are running to and fro on every hand. This, says the Word of God, indicates the time of the end. One simply cannot ignore the significance of these words "many shall run to and fro."

INCREASE OF KNOWLEDGE

Accompanying this increase in travel, Daniel says, "knowledge shall be increased." We see signs of this development everywhere around us. Since the industrial revolution of the 19th century, our knowledge has increased as by a miracle. The machine age has brought in innumerable innovations. We have gone from the sickle to the combine in a few brief years, from the ox team to the multi-bladed gang plow and the caterpillar tractor in a generation, from the horse and buggy to the jet plane in half a lifetime. Now, our discovery of atomic energy, with all its possibilities, promises increase in knowledge and speed in travel such as man has never dreamed of before.

Not only has knowledge increased in the field of invention and discovery, but also in the field of education. A few years ago an eighth grade education was really something. Few went on to high school. Today, illiteracy is almost unknown, high school educations are for everybody and many more are receiving college educations as a requirement for jobs and occupations which formerly demanded no preparation whatsoever.

The increase of knowledge in medicine and surgery is indescribable. Such scourges as small pox, diphtheria, scarlet fever and typhoid are almost unknown. Today, there is a wealth of knowledge concerning drugs and medicines, antibiotics and vitamins. The progress in surgery, especially heart surgery, and the advance in the conquest of almost every disease is phenomenal. Think how knowledge has increased concerning the structure of matter in the discovery of atomic fission and the greatly increased knowledge of the heavens in astronomy. This advance is true of every field of knowledge.

KNOWLEDGE OF THE WORD

A phenomenal increase has come about in the field of Bible knowledge. Many things have been learned in regard to the interpretations of the content of the Scriptures, especially in the field of prophecy and the signs of the Lord's return, which were closed and dark before. This is what Daniel meant when he said it would be shut up and sealed until the time of the end. At that time the truths of the Word would be revealed, just before the Lord's return. That day is here. In the light of all this we can but marvel at the inspired statement that, at the time of the end, "many shall run to and fro, and knowledge shall be increased."

There are many other signs of Christ's soon return, the strange sights in the heavens of the past few years, flying saucers, meteors, smoke palls and other peculiar happenings. Add to this the freakish storms, the frequency of earthquakes and hurricanes. All these remind us of the words of Jesus in Luke 21:25-26,

> And there shall be signs in the sun, and in the moon, and in the stars; and upon the earth distress of nations, with perplexity; the sea and the waves roaring;
> Men's hearts failing them for fear, and for looking after those things which are coming on the earth: for the powers of heaven shall be shaken.

Is there a more perfect description of the days in which we live? Yet, these words were spoken by Jesus over nineteen hundred years ago. Yes, He is coming again. The important question now is, Are you ready? Christians, if you knew how little time there is left, how you would busy yourselves to make each day count for God and to get the Gospel out! Sinners, if you knew how soon you will have to answer before God for your rejection of Christ, how you would flee from the wrath to come!

> He which testifieth these things saith, Surely I come quickly. Amen. Even so, come, Lord Jesus (Rev. 22:20).

CHAPTER SIX

Be Not Deceived

> And while they looked stedfastly toward heaven as he
> went up, behold, two men stood by them in white apparel;
>   Which also said, Ye men of Galilee, why stand ye
> gazing up into heaven? this same Jesus, which is taken up
> from you into heaven, shall so come in like manner as ye
> have seen him go into heaven (Acts 1:10-11).

These are the last words of our Lord and Saviour Jesus
Christ to His disciples and waiting Church, just before He
ascended into heaven. From these words we know there is no
event more certain and more sure than the return of the
Lord Jesus Christ. His return is more certain than death itself,
for the Scripture says,

> . . . We shall not all sleep, but we shall all be
> changed,
>   In a moment, in the twinkling of an eye . . . (I Corin-
> thians 15:51-52).

When the Lord Jesus Christ comes, there will be a company
of believers who will never taste death, for they will "all be
changed in a moment, in the twinkling of an eye, at the last
trump." "For the trumpet shall sound and the dead shall be
raised incorruptible, and we shall all be changed" (I Corinthians 15:52).

This is called in Scripture "that blessed hope." It is the hope
of the dead in Christ, that they shall be raised incorruptible
upon His return. David says,

> . . . my flesh also shall rest in hope. For thou wilt not
> leave my soul in sheol; neither wilt thou suffer thine Holy
> One to see corruption (Psalm 16:9-10).

This prayer of David's is pre-eminently the hope of those who will still be alive at the return of the Lord Jesus. It is, especially for them, "that blessed hope," for it means that those who are alive at His coming shall never experience death, but will be caught up, transformed in a moment, in the twinkling of an eye, in His own precious image.

All true believers, therefore, are intensely interested in this momentous future event, the most dramatic since Calvary. We should search the Scriptures carefully for every bit of information concerning that great event and seek to determine the "times and the seasons" of His soon return. While we are definitely warned against the setting of dates, we are just as severely warned not to be ignorant of the signs of His coming. Jesus castigated and criticized the scribes and the Pharisees for not being able to read the signs of the times. That His disciples might not make the same mistake, He gave them, shortly before He went to Calvary, a long list of signs which would precede His wonderful coming again.

MATTHEW 24

Among the many passages recording the teaching of our Lord concerning the signs of His return, the most detailed and clearest is found in Matthew 24. A careful study of this great prophetic chapter should be made by all who would know the "signs of the times" and the nearness of the return of the Lord Jesus Christ. The whole chapter is our Lord's response to a question by the disciples in Matthew 24:3. The disciples had asked, ". . . as he sat upon the mount of Olives . . . Tell us, when shall these things be? and what shall be the sign of thy coming, and the end of the world?"

Before looking at these signs which follow, I would like to emphasize two things in this verse. *First of all,* notice that these words were spoken privately to the disciples. This is not a public address by the Lord Jesus to the multitudes, but a message for the disciples only. The unconverted need another message, a message which looks backward, not forward to His coming again. Until the unsaved go back to the Cross, the Second Coming of the Lord Jesus has no comfort for them, nor can they be expected to be interested in it, or to understand it. If one who professes to be a believer, therefore, expresses no interest in the return of the Lord Jesus Christ, he may well question whether he is saved at all. Remember that this message will be of comfort only to born-again believers. To all others the coming of Christ means only judgment and everlasting remorse after He comes to judge the wicked.

The second thing to note in this verse is that He is speaking of His coming and the end of the world. The coming again of the Lord Jesus Christ is linked with the end of the world in this passage. Unfortunately, a faulty translation of this verse has caused many to be confused concerning the end of the world and the coming again of Christ. The last word in this verse (Matthew 24:3) is "world" in the King James Version. The word in the original Greek is "aionos," which corresponds to our English word "eon." It means "age" or "dispensation." It never should have been translated "world." My pulpit commentary translates the phrase thus, "What shall be the sign of thy coming, and the consummation of the age?" The word translated "coming" is "parousias," the word consistently used throughout the Scriptures for the "arrival" and the "coming again" of the Lord Jesus Christ. The end of this age, then, will come when the Lord Jesus Christ Himself returns.

IT IS NOT THE END OF THE WORLD

This is *not* to be confused with the "end of the world." The end of the "age" and the end of the "world" are two *entirely different* events, separated by a great period of time. The end of the world will not occur until at least one thousand years after the end of this present age to which our Lord Jesus Christ refers in this passage. The end of the "age" will come when our Lord returns for His Church. After a brief period of the Tribulation, He will cleanse the earth and judge His enemies. Then, our Lord will set up His Messianic, millennial kingdom upon the earth. After that, at the end of the thousand years, Satan will stage his last, final rebellion, only to be destroyed immediately with his followers by fire falling from heaven. Then comes the "end of the world" as described in II Peter 3:12. The Lord will create a new heaven and a new earth "wherein dwelleth righteousness" (II Peter 3:13).

The end of the *age*, therefore, may occur at any time when the Lord Jesus Christ comes again. The end of the *world,* on the other hand, will come only after the Millennium, at the end of time and the beginning of eternity. One can never understand prophecy or the signs of the coming again of Christ without being able to distinguish between these two events, "the end of the *age"* and "the end of the *world."*

THE ANSWER OF JESUS

Here is the answer of our Lord to His disciples question concerning His coming again, and the end of this age: "And Jesus answered and said unto them, Take heed that no man deceive you" (Matthew 24:4). This verse is both a sign and a solemn warning. The last days, says our Saviour, will be a time of deception. It is a significant fact that the first of the many signs in this passage is a warning against the deceptions of men concerning the return of Christ. How significant, I repeat, when we consider the confusion of tongues in religious circles in these days in which we live. Never before in all history have there been such divisions in Christendom. There are today over 350 different denominations, sects and cults in Protestantism in America alone. All of these claim that they are right and that all others are necessarily wrong. One says this and another says that, until men cry out in sincerity, "What can we believe about these things? Who, after all, is right? Where is the truth found?" Jesus answers those questions in this first warning: "Take heed that no *man* deceive you." The test is this: Is it the Word of God or the opinion of a man? Only as we turn to the Word of God can we be sure that we have not been deceived by men.

It is said that a new cult or sect springs up at least once a month in the United States, and that no matter how fantastic and fanatical its teachings may be, or how wild its claims, there are always those who are willing to be deceived. How timely therefore, is the warning of our Lord Jesus Christ, "Take heed that no man deceive you."

After our Saviour has issued this warning, He adds at least nine more important signs in the next few verses of Matthew 24. They are as follows:

And Jesus answered and said unto them, Take heed that no man deceive you.

For many shall come in my name, saying, I am Christ; and shall deceive many.

And ye shall hear of wars and rumours of wars: see that ye be not troubled: for all these things must come to pass, but the end is not yet.

For nation shall rise against nation, and kingdom against kingdom; and there shall be famines, and pestilences, and earthquakes, in divers places.

All these are the beginning of sorrows.

Then shall they deliver you up to be afflicted, and shall kill you: and ye shall be hated of all nations for my name's sake.

And then shall many be offended, and shall betray one another, and shall hate one another.

And many false prophets shall rise, and shall deceive many.

And because iniquity shall abound, the love of many shall wax cold.

But he that shall endure unto the end, the same shall be saved.

And this gospel of the kingdom shall be preached in all the world for a witness unto all nations; and then shall the end come (Matthew 24:4-14).

There are a number of signs which the Lord Jesus Christ mentions in this passage. I shall enumerate them for you as follows:

1. Increase of deception
2. False christs
3. Wars and rumors of wars
4. Famines and pestilences
5. Simultaneous earthquakes
6. Racial intolerance and persecution
7. Independability of men
8. False prophets
9. Apostasy
10. Universal preaching of the Gospel of the kingdom

Here, then, are ten signs, including the one of deception which will characterize the end of the age and the return of Christ. If you are inclined to find fault with these, just remember that you are criticizing the Lord Jesus Christ, for these are the words of our Saviour Himself in answer to the question of the disciples, "What shall be the sign of thy coming, and the end of the age?"

The objection is perennially raised that all these signs mentioned by Jesus have been present throughout this entire dispensation. Men tell us there have always been false messiahs, wars, pestilences, famines, earthquakes and race strife, apostasy and violence. This is only partly true, however. The last of these signs, the universal preaching of the gospel has never before been possible in history as it is today. The last one of these signs, the universal preaching of the Gospel, therefore, has been fulfilled in these very days in which we are living.

There is yet another point to be emphasized. While all these ten signs in Matthew 24:3-14, with the exception of the last one, have occurred throughout history, they have never

been present, all of them, at one and the same time. I repeat, never before have all these signs occurred simultaneously.
It was the Lord Jesus Himself who said, "So likewise ye, when
ye shall see *all* these things, know that it is near, even at the
doors" (Matthew 24:33).

We, therefore, assert confidently that His coming is drawing
near. For the first time in history all these signs are present
at one and the same time. How important, then, to face the
most pressing question, "Are you ready for the coming of the
Lord?" When He comes, the door of salvation will be closed
forever to all who have heard the invitation but have wilfully
refused to accept it. Trust Him *now* and be saved.

CHAPTER SEVEN

Will Conditions Get Better?

Tell us, when shall these things be? and what shall
be the sign of thy coming, and of the end of the
world (Matthew 24:3)

The twenty-fourth chapter of Matthew is the answer of
our Lord Jesus Christ to this question of His disciples concerning His coming the second time. Our Saviour was nearing
the end of His earthly ministry and had been encouraging
the hearts of His disciples with the sure promise that, although He was going to leave them, He was also coming back.
Naturally, the hearts of the disciples were anxious to know
when He would return. Hence this question, "Tell us,
when shall these things be?"

TEN SIGNS

Then, Jesus answers their questions. In the first fourteen
verses of Matthew 24, He gives ten definite signs, which,
when they come to pass, He says, will establish the nearness of
His return and the end of this present age or dispensation.
These ten signs, as we have already seen, were:

1. Increase of deception
2. False christs
3. Wars and rumors of wars
4. Famines and pestilences
5. Simultaneous earthquakes
6. Racial intolerance and persecution
7. Independability of man
8. False prophets

9. Apostasy

10. Universal preaching of the Gospel of the kingdom

We must be content to point out just a few thoughts concerning each of these signs.

We have already seen that there will be great deception at the end of the age, especially concerning the truth of the Lord's return. It is, therefore, noteworthy that almost all the passages in Scripture which deal with the truth of the Second Coming of Christ are accompanied by a solemn warning against being deceived by men concerning these matters. The Lord Jesus knew all the false interpretations, the denials, the perversions, which Satan would foist upon men and women concerning this blessed, encouraging truth. The devil knows that the truth of the imminent return of Christ is a stimulating, comforting, energizing, purifying hope. He would rob us of its blessing by causing all sorts of confusion among believers, one crying this thing and another saying that thing. Some would deny His coming altogether; others would delay His coming again until after the Tribulation or at the end of the world; others would seek to debauch it by all sorts of foolish, fanatical and fantastical interpretations and unscriptural predictions. As a result of this confusion, many Christians know not what to believe. That is why they ignore and refuse to study this subject at all. They say, "There is so much difference of opinion among believers that we do not know what is the truth." So they ignore this truth and impoverish their own lives.

That is exactly what the devil wants all of us to do. He wants us just to forget about the Second Coming truth, as though it, after all, is not an important or basic or fundamental doctrine at all, in spite of the fact that it occupies a larger place in Scripture than any other single doctrine. Jesus, therefore, warns us to "Take heed that *no man* deceive you." Be on guard, on the look-out, says our Saviour, for human de-

ceptions and human interpretations. The only remedy against
these forces is to turn away from all of man's opinion and
limit ourselves entirely to the Word of God. What does the
Scripture say is the final test? That will give us the answer.

FALSE CHRISTS

After this warning, Jesus gives the second sign which would
characterize the end of the age, false christs. "Many shall
come in my name saying, I am Christ; and shall deceive
many" (Matthew 24:5). I am told that, in the past fifty
years, no less than eleven hundred leaders, great and small, in
various parts of the world, have claimed to be the Christ and
the Saviour of the world. They have called themselves by the
names of God, Divine Fathers, the Great I Am's and a thousand other movements claiming the perogatives of Christ and
of deity. All of them have claimed deluded followers by the
thousands in fulfillment of Jesus' words, "and they shall deceive many."

OTHER SIGNS

The third sign which Jesus gives is that of wars and rumors
of wars. If you object and say, "there have always been wars
and rumors of wars," let me remind you that it has never
been like it is today. You may read all of history; you will
find no precedent for the conditions in the world as we see
them right now. In my own brief lifetime, there have been
two world wars, not counting the scores of lesser wars all
over the world. Today, we are facing the greatest of all, an
atomic world war.

The next mentioned sign (the fourth) is famines and
pestilences. While there have always been famines and there
have always been pestilences, this past generation has seen
them in greater intensity than ever before. Though some
nations are at a loss as to what to do with their surplus food,
millions are starving in India, in China and in Europe.
Millions of bushels of potatoes have been fed to cattle and

others turned into fuel. Countless crates of eggs have been dried and stored and now have no market value whatsoever. Yet, there are millions of people who are dying for the lack of these things, so abundant in our land that we are at a loss to know what to do with them. Jesus predicted all these things. Never before in history has famine been as intense as it is today.

The Lord next mentions earthquakes. Again I hear someone say, "There have always been earthquakes." That is true, but science tells us there have never been as many earthquakes as there have been in these recent years. Seismologists tell us that the earth is in an almost constant state of tremor, that earthquakes of varying intensity are occurring several times each day. It is almost impossible to pick up any issue of our newspapers without a report of an earthquake or a tremor somewhere in the world. The real point in Jesus' prediction, however, lies in the last three words of this verse concerning earthquakes, Matthew 24:7. These three words are, "in divers places." The suggestion is that several earthquakes will occur simultaneously in different parts of the world. This, too, had never before been reported until within the last ten or fifteen years, when as many as three major quakes have occurred on three widely separated continents at the same time. For the first time in history, therefore, these words of our Lord Jesus, "earthquakes in divers places," have been literally fulfilled.

THE BEGINNING OF SORROWS

The next verse (Matthew 24:8) is an important verse because it marks a division. "All these are the beginning of sorrows." This verse divides the passage we are studying into two parts, at the first of which we have already been looking. When these first events take place they are the beginning of the end. Still other signs will follow which the Lord gives here. These signs are racial hatred, especially anti-semitism.

Verse 9 says, "Then shall they deliver you up to be afflicted." This refers especially to the nation of Israel, the nation to which these disciples themselves belonged.

Here let me give a word of explanation. All of these things described in this passage in Matthew 24 reach their climax and their highest intensity *during the Tribulation, after the Rapture* of the Church. This twenty-fourth chapter of Matthew deals primarily with the Tribulation period. Therefore, all these signs will reach their complete fulfillment and culmination only after the Church has been taken out and the Day of the Lord has set in here upon the earth. The Rapture, we believe, will precede the public Second Coming of Christ by at least seven years. In between the Rapture and His public appearance will come the Tribulation period. These signs which the Lord gives are the signs *not primarily* of the Rapture, but they *are* the signs of His Second Coming to the earth *after* the Rapture and *after* the Tribulation. Since the Rapture is to be seven years prior to His Second Coming to earth, and the signs indicating the nearness of this Second Coming to earth after the Tribulation are already in the process of fulfillment, we can imagine how near the Rapture itself must be, when it occurs seven years before the Tribulation. I repeat, however, the complete fulfillment of these signs in Matthew 24 will occur *after* the Church is translated. If, they are already beginning to take place we may confidently say that the Rapture must be nearer than most of us realize.

TREASON AND DISHONESTY

The next sign (the seventh) which Jesus mentions is treason and dishonesty among men (Matthew 24:10). He says, "And then shall many be offended, and shall betray one another, and shall hate one another." We have but to call attention to the dishonesty of the nations, the broken pacts and covenants, the secret commitments which have been made, the fifth column activities, the traitors within our own gates, feeding upon our own abundance, serving a foreign power and seeking the overthrow of our democracy. All these facts are well known to every one of us.

Next, Jesus mentions false prophets. They are to be distinguished from false christs and false teachers. These prophets claim to speak for God but serve the devil instead. They would beguile us with enticing words, assuring us that all is well and that we will ultimately fix up this old world without the necessity of the return of Christ. There are false prophets who set dates, false prophets who tell us Jesus has already returned somewhere in the past, false prophets who would have us believe we are now already in the Tribulation or in the Millennium.

Apostasy and indifference are the next signs mentioned. "Because iniquity shall abound, the love of many shall wax cold" (Matthew 24:12). Never before in human history has this been as true as it is today. In a few brief decades we have departed from the simple faith of the Puritan fathers to a place where Christ is almost entirely crowded out of our public, social and economic life. Christ is banned from our schools, from our national assemblies, from our political meetings, our business life and from much of society. The Name of Jesus Christ is banned and taboo because of the offense to infidels. We like to be called a Christian nation, but it is hard to find Christ in much of our social, educational or political life today. Even among Christians it is too tragically true that "the love of many shall wax cold." The love of many *has* waxed cold.

Endure to the End

The Lord Jesus adds a statement in verse 13 which has caused untold confusion because many misunderstand its setting. Here is the controversial verse: "But he that shall endure unto the end, the same shall be saved." Many have interpreted this as applying to the Christians living now before the Rapture. As we stated before, on the contrary, this entire passage deals particularly with the Tribulation period. The signs in Matthew 24 while now already beginning, will be consummated only *after* the Rapture and *during* the Tribulation period. It is to those living then, in the Tribulation, that these words apply, "He that shall endure to the end, the same shall be saved." Those who in that day have the seal of the living God, and not the mark of the beast, shall not perish in the Tribulation as others will, but will be saved from the awful plagues and the death of the Day of the Lord and the judgment of the Tribulation.

How Near That Day Must Be!

Though these signs are signs of His Second Coming, we who wait for the Rapture may read and understand them clearly. Seeing these signs and telling of the soon coming of Jesus to set up His kingdom encourages our hearts. We know that His coming for us must be even nearer, for we shall be caught up before that terrible day shall come. One of these days it is going to happen. Men may scoff, they may laugh, they may make fun of it, they may ignore it, but just as sure as God is true, Jesus Christ *is* coming again. The important question is this, "Are you ready for His return?" You can prepare yourself right now by turning to Him, and trusting His promise,

Believe on the Lord Jesus Christ and thou shalt be saved.

CHAPTER EIGHT

A Warning to Hypocrites

When it is evening, ye say, It will be fair weather; for the sky is red.

And in the morning, It will be foul weather to day: for the sky is red and lowring. O ye hypocrites, ye can discern the face of the sky; but can ye not discern the signs of the times? (Matthew 16:2-3)

"Red at night means sailor's delight; red in the morning is the sailor's warning." Thus runs the old proverb paraphrasing the words of the Lord Jesus spoken in this passage to the hypocritical Pharisees of His day when they asked Him for a sign from heaven. These are the words of the Lord Jesus Christ as He berated the educated and intellectual Pharisees and the leaders of Israel for not recognizing Him as the Messiah and the Christ of God. All of the prophets of the Old Testament had predicted in great detail the First Coming of Jesus Christ. When He Came, He came in fulfillment of scores and scores of plain prophecies. One wonders how anyone could have missed recognizing Him as the One who had been promised.

The Old Testament had predicted how the Messiah would come from Bethlehem in Judea, born of a virgin, how that He would manifest Himself by many signs and wonders, healing the sick, casting out demons, raising the dead and preaching the Gospel of peace. Yet in spite of all the prophecies concerning Him, and all the wonders and miracles and signs which He performed, these leaders of Israel never even recognized Him as the Son of God. In spite of all the evidences of His divine Person and Mission, they still asked Him for another sign from heaven. To this demand of unbelief, Jesus answers, "Ye know how to read the sky for the weather forecast, but ye have overlooked all the signs which pointed to My coming and My ministry." These leaders of Israel were the ones who should have been the first to recognize Him and to introduce Him to the people. Instead, these who should have known the Scripture rejected Him and the common people received Him.

The Same Is True of His Second Coming

While the primary application of Jesus' words, therefore, is to His *First Coming*, it is just as applicable to His *Second Coming*, for there are far more signs given to indicate His Second Coming than there were concerning His First Coming. The Bible has a great deal more to say about the Second Advent of Christ than about His First Coming into the world. The Old Testament prophet saw very little of the First Coming, but chapter after chapter deals with His glorious Second Coming. If the leaders of Israel were rebuked and berated for failing to interpret the relatively few prophecies concerning His First Advent, what will He do with those of us who live in this enlightened age and yet utterly ignore and fail to interpret the greater volume of signs concerning His Second Coming to the earth? It may be said today as it was said in the days gone by, "O ye hypocrites, ye can discern the face of the sky, but can ye not discern the signs of the times?"

The Bible Is Full of Signs

Jesus had a great deal to say about the signs of His Second Coming. As He approached the Cross of His rejection, He began to speak more and more about His return to this earth in vindication of His rejection and humiliating death at the First Advent. In Matthew, His last words before the Cross were almost entirely about His return. The same is true of

Mark and Luke and of John. The first message of Christ which He sent back by the two men on the Mount of the Ascension was, "This same Jesus who has gone up from you into heaven shall so come in like manner as ye have seen him go away" (Acts1:11). Throughout the epistles, with almost no exception, the hope set before the believer is His return the second time. The final book of the Bible deals almost exclusively with the fact and the events preceding, accompanying and following this glorious event, *the Second Coming of Christ.*

We Cannot Know the Day Nor the Hour

The time of Christ's return for His Church is not known to any one. All attempts to fix dates or hours are a delusion, a snare and are un-scriptural. All predictions concerning the exact moment of Christ's return are false and born either of ignorance or an attempt to deceive for the purpose of attracting attention or publicity. The Christian should shun all those who attempt to set dates for the return of the Lord.

After having said this, we have not said all that the Scripture states on this particular subject, for, while the Bible does warn against setting the day and the hour, it also definitely tells us that we may know approximately the time and the season of His return. As the signs He has given multiply, we may, with confidence, tell men and women that His coming is very near and that we are living in the days when the Lord will soon return. The Apostle Paul, in writing concerning the return of the Lord Jesus, tells us plainly in I Thessalonians 5,

> But of the times and the seasons, brethren, ye have no need that I write unto you.
>
> For yourselves know perfectly that the day of the Lord so cometh as a thief in the night.
>
> For when they shall say, Peace and safety; then sudden destruction cometh upon them, as travail upon a woman with child; and they shall not escape.

> But ye, brethren, are not in darkness, that that day
> should overtake you as a thief.
> Ye are all the children of light, and the children of the
> day: we are not of the night, nor of the darkness.
> Therefore let us not sleep, as do others; but let us watch
> and be sober   (I Thessalonians 5:1-6).

This is a passage which has been tragically overlooked by many Christians. It tells us that while the coming of Christ will surprise the world, as a thief, it will in no way be a surprise to the children of God who know the Bible and the signs of the times. Paul states clearly that while we may not fix the day nor the hour, we *can* know the times and the seasons. While the coming of the Lord will be wholly unexpected and a complete surprise to the world, it should not be so for us if we will but study our Bibles. To illustrate this, Paul uses the very striking figure of an expectant mother. We may know approximately the time of a child's birth, but the exact day and hour cannot be predicted by even the most learned obstetrician. As the day of birth approaches, however, we can set the approximate time within more or less narrow limits, as to the delivery. We can know about the season, or the time, but as to the exact hour or the day, this remains a secret. Now, that is the figure which Paul uses very interestingly in discussing the time of Christ's return. He says, we do not know the date or the day, but we may know the times and the seasons and have been sufficiently informed as to the signs which will indicate the time of Christ's coming again. Today, for the first time in history, all of these signs are with us. As each day passes without His return and the signs increase in intensity, we can say each day, with greater emphasis and greater certainty, that we are living nearer to the end time. We have a right to expect the return of our Lord Jesus Christ at any moment.

MANY, MANY SIGNS

In this passage in I Thessalonians, Paul mentions one significant sign of Christ's return among the hundreds of others found throughout the rest of the Bible. It is found in verse 3, "For when they shall say, Peace and safety; then sudden destruction cometh upon them . . . " (I Thessalonians 5:3).

A passage like that needs little comment in these days of peace conferences and other organizations which have been set up for the express purpose of bringing world peace. Never before has there been more talk of peace. Yet, never before has there been more fear and threat of war. There are more men under arms throughout the world today than in any other period of so-called peace time in all of the world's history. All we hear is peace, fighting to maintain peace and police protection to preserve peace. At the same time we hear of war and threatenings of war, bickering among the nations, maneuvering for power, clever manipulations of power politics and a race for spheres of influence throughout the world. The international deliberations of today are following the pattern laid down in the Scriptures for these last days, "when they shall say Peace and safety; then shall sudden destruction come upon them . . . "

The Bible clearly states that there can be no lasting world peace until the Prince of Peace, the Lord Jesus Christ, returns. The Bible is full of incontrovertible evidence that this age will not end in peace, but in war, the greatest of all wars, the battle of Armageddon. Jesus said the last days would be characterized by wars and rumors of wars, nations rising up against nation, in the greatest armament race of all history. Daniel 9, verse 26, is a significant verse. Speaking of the course of this age, Daniel says, " . . . and unto the end of the war desolations are determined." This verse literally should read, "And unto the end wars and desolations are determined." I would have you notice one word particularly. It is the

word "determined." God says that until the Messiah comes
again, wars and desolations are determined. That is what the
Almighty says. All efforts of peace, therefore, without the
Prince of Peace, must prove futile and vain in the end.

The Bible definitely teaches that until the Lord Jesus comes
again there can be no lasting peace or universal acceptance of
the Gospel. That is not the program of God. All who teach
that the world will gradually become better and better through
the discoveries of science, the progress of learning and education, by reformation and conferences and the preaching of
a social gospel of good works, are going contrary to what we
believe to be the clear statement of the Word of God in regard to the course of this present age. Yet, today, there are
an increasing number of individuals and organizations spring-
ing up everywhere who tell us of the glorious future of this
world, without the necessity of the return of the Prince of
Peace, the Lord Jesus. The sad, sad thing is that millions are
being deceived by this will-of-the-wisp of man's Utopian,
Christ-less dreaming. It is all a deception and a delusion of
the enemy of God and Christ. The Bible states clearly that
this age will end in apostasy, not in revival, and spiritual
declension," not in moral perfection and religious awakening.

ALL INDICATIONS ARE BEING FULFILLED

Without an exception, every single passage of Scripture,
which deals with conditions just before the coming again of
Christ, teaches that it will be a time of violence, wickedness,
godlessness and apostasy. One has but to study the days of
Noah to find out how like our age today was the time of
which Jesus said, "But as the days of Noe were, so shall
also the coming of the Son of man be" (Matthew 24:37).
The whole moral fabric of the world has broken down. The
sacredness of marriage is all but gone. Divorce is respectable
today, whereas it was a disgrace only a generation ago.
Drunkenness is at an all-time high. Profanity and cursing are

no longer considered vulgar. A decent, respectable citizen shudders at the thought of travel, for one can hardly go anywhere, in the train, on the bus or in any public place, without being forced to listen to cursing and swearing and vile talk which makes one's blood run cold. A few years ago, when we spoke to people about their language, they would apologize and feel ashamed. Today, when we rebuke these blasphemers who take the Name of the Lord in vain, it only serves to set loose a greater volume of profanity. Profanity and blasphemy are accepted today without objection, even in much of our literature. In the magazines and periodicals and public addresses of leaders and officials we are made to listen to God's Name being used in vain.

Add to this the increase in juvenile delinquency, the amazing increase in crime and violence. We have a repetition of the days of Noah. We have but to go back twenty-five years in our own memories to see the rapidity with which our sense of morals and decency has abated and declined. Things are accepted today as perfectly all right and proper for which a man could have been put in prison twenty-five years ago. Certainly the experience of man is in full harmony with the Word of God, that until the end these things will continue to become worse, and that there can be no real lasting peace, relief or righteousness until the Prince of Peace comes again. That is why we continue to preach the coming again of Jesus Christ. We repeat it for just two reasons—first, the Bible tells us He *is* coming again, and all the indications and signs point to His soon return; second, there is no hope for this old world without the Lord Jesus Christ.

Even so, come, Lord Jesus.

CHAPTER NINE

Fearful Sights in Heaven

> But as the days of Noe were, so shall also the coming of the Son of man be.
>
> For as in the days that were before the flood they were eating and drinking, marrying and giving in marriage, until the day that Noe entered into the ark,
>
> And knew not until the flood came, and took them all away; so shall also the coming of the Son of man be.
>
> Then shall two be in the field; the one shall be taken, and the other left.
>
> Two women shall be grinding at the mill; the one shall be taken, and the other left.
>
> Watch therefore: for ye know not what hour your Lord doth come   (Matthew 24:37-42).

The surest, most certain thing in all the world is the actual, literal Second Coming of the Lord Jesus Christ at the end of this age. Just as surely as He came to this earth the first time nineteen hundred years ago, just so surely is He coming again. The same prophets who predicted His literal First Coming also prophesied at the same time His literal Second Coming. The same infallible Holy Spirit who inspired these prophets to foretell His First Coming also moved upon these same men at the same time to predict His Second Coming. His First Coming was literal, He came a literal man, born of a literal mother, born in a literal stable and was visited by literal shepherds and wise men. No one is foolish enough to deny the literal fulfillment of the events connected with His First Coming. Yet people will argue away the prophecies of His Second Coming by trying to make them spiritual and thus get rid of this important teaching of the Word of God. The literalness of Christ's First Coming demands the same for His Second. The promise right after He left was, "Ye men of Galilee, why stand ye gazing up into heaven? this same Jesus, which is taken up from you into heaven, shall so come in like manner as ye have seen him go into heaven" (Acts 1:11).

This one passage alone should convince anyone with an open mind of the certainty and the literalness of the return of the Lord Jesus.

In previous pages we have seen a number of signs which Jesus gave to His disciples as He sat on the Mount of Olives in answer to their question concerning the signs of His return. We turn now to the parallel passage found in Luke 21. Doctor Luke repeats many of the signs given in Matthew 24 and Mark 13, but adds a number of other signs, often overlooked, and not mentioned in Matthew and in Mark. He mentions, in Luke 21:11, certain occurrences in the heavens when he says,

> And great earthquakes shall be in divers places, and famines, and pestilences; and fearful sights and great signs shall there be from heaven.

FEARFUL SIGHTS

Jesus said that these latter days would be characterized by fearful sights and great signs in the heavens. None of us, I am sure, fail to see the reference to the many strange things which have been happening, especially of late. Surely there are strange goings on today in the heavens. Man has already unlocked the secret of the atom; he is experimenting with cosmic energy; he is seeking to discover the secret of gravitational powers which hold the universe together. We hear of flying saucers and visitors from other planets. Man talks freely of interplanetary travel and trips to the moon, smoke palls covering several states, causing the darkness of night at midday, freak storms and flashing lights in the heavens which no one seems to be able or willing to explain. They tell us these lights are great meteors, but they are never found. One recently exploded atomic bomb caused a light so intense that it lit up cities four hundred miles away from the blast. The light was seen in a fraction of a second, the rumble of explosion came many minutes later. Strange things, indeed, are happening in the heavens today.

Distress of Nations

Our Lord Jesus Christ adds still more information in Luke 21, verse 25, when He says,

> And there shall be signs in the sun, and in the moon, and in the stars; and upon the earth distress of nations with perplexity; the sea and the waves roaring.

Three additional signs are mentioned here:

1. Distress of nations
2. Perplexity of nations
3. Unprecedented storms

First of all, notice the distress of nations. It is amazing that these words were spoken two thousand years ago by our Saviour. What better description could anyone give of the present international situation among the peoples of the world. "The nations in distress" seems to sum up the whole story. A few years ago we dreamed of one world, we hailed the U.N. as the solution of the problems of war and international relationships. Now we have two worlds, an East and a West, freedom and slavery, democracy and totalitarianism. No one has yet found an answer. The nations are distressed. There is no more distressed company of people today than the members of the United Nations and those in places of great authority, as they seek for a solution which no one seems to be able to bring.

Our Lord Jesus Christ adds the words "with perplexity." *With Perplexity.* To be perplexed is to be without a solution or an answer. There is no word in the English language

which better describes the dilemma of our diplomats, statesmen
and leaders today. One says this, another suggests that. Still
another suggests something else. All these are sincere, we
believe, but with as widely different suggestions for a solution as it is possible for anyone to imagine. The Lord Jesus
Christ adds still more and says, "the sea and the waves
roaring." The past few years have seen some of the most
destructive storms and floods of all history. Even the weather
seems to be perplexed. You may shrug off these things, you
may ignore them, you may laugh at all of them, but let me
remind you, these are the words of the Lord Jesus Christ
spoken in all seriousness. Any one of these things by itself
may not have much significance and may be called coin-
cidences. Taken together, however, they add up to just one
thing—the beginning of the fulfillment of the signs of the
times.

These signs in Matthew, Mark and Luke are signs of
Christ's Second Coming at the close of the Tribulation period.
Since we confidently believe that the Lord Jesus will come for
His Church *before* the Tribulation, it makes these signs even
more significant. Some one has aptly said, "Signs are for the
nation of Israel." God has given no signs to the Church.
The Bible very definitely says that "the Jews require a sign,
and the Greeks seek after wisdom: but we preach Christ
crucified . . . " (I Corinthians 2:22). All of this is true. It
is very well to believe these things, but the fact that these are
signs of His coming to the earth after the Day of the Lord
given particularly to the nation of Israel does not in any way
prevent us from reading these signs.

A sign along the road may not be for me at all, but I
certainly can read it. I drive along the highway and I see a
sign which reads, "Turn here for the boilermaker's picnic."
I am not a boiler maker and I am not going to their picnic.
I have no business there. This does not prevent me from
reading the sign and knowing where and when the boiler

makers are going to come together for their picnic. So, too, with the signs of the return of the Lord Jesus Christ to the earth. Although you may insist that these signs are primarily for the Tribulation period and Israel, and will come about only after the Church is raptured and point only to the Second Coming of the Lord Jesus Christ, I do thank God that I can still read the signs and know how near we are to that day.

There is, therefore, no excuse for anyone to be ignorant of the meaning of these signs of the times. May God help us to be on the alert, and to be like the wise householder who will not be surprised by the thief.

In the light of all this revelation of the Word of God, and the events which today are pointing to the soon return of our precious Saviour, how solemn we should be, how busy to make the most of every opportunity to witness for our Lord and Saviour, Jesus Christ! Certainly the Lord could not have made His Word any plainer than He has. We have given you a large number of signs which Jesus Himself gave by which we might know how late it is on God's clock. We cannot take these things lightly. We must take them seriously. There are many other indications besides these which are mentioned in the Word of God. One of the most profitable exercises for the child of God today is to search the Scriptures and to see how near the coming of the Lord must truly be. One of these days we as Christians will have to meet that Saviour who gave His all for us that we might have eternal life. We shall have to give an accounting to Him not only of how we have lived, but of how we have used the opportunities and talents entrusted to our cares. May the Lord grant us to heed the words of Scripture, "Seeing then that all these things shall be dissolved, what manner of persons ought ye to be in all holy conversation and godliness" (II Peter 3:11).

May the Lord grant us that when He shall come, whether it be at noon or night, we may not be ashamed at His appearing but may have an abundant entrance into the kingdom of light and of His eternal peace.

For those of you who are still unsaved without the Lord Jesus Christ, there can be nothing ahead but only judgment. What excuse can you offer Him when He comes to judge the earth and the inhabitants of the earth? You certainly cannot claim ignorance, for you have once again heard the "thus saith the Lord." If you had never heard the Gospel it would not be nearly as terrible for you in that day, because added light rejected will mean added responsibility and judgment. It were better never to have heard the invitation of the Gospel, than to have heard it and then to reject it. Jesus laid down an eternal principle in Luke 12 when He said,

> That servant, which knew his Lord's will, and prepared not himself, neither did according to his will, shall be beaten with many stripes.
>
> But he that knew not, and did commit things worthy of stripes, shall be beaten with few stripes. For unto whomsoever much is given, of him shall be much required: and to whom men have committed much, of him they will ask the more (Luke 12:47-48).

You cannot escape the Gospel once you have heard it. It is to you either a savor of life unto life if you believe it, or a savor of death unto death if you reject it. Receive Christ *now*, believe His promise and be saved. He Himself said, "Him that cometh to me I will in no wise cast out" (John 6:37).

In conclusion, we want to sound this two-fold warning again. First of all, to you who are believers, there can be no question in the sincere Bible student's mind as to the fact that we are rapidly approaching the time when the Lord Jesus Christ will return and we will have to give an account to Him of how we have spent our time and our talents and our energy and how much we have acquainted ourselves with His program while it is still called today. May the Lord grant us all to catch the vision, that the days are short and evil, that the King's business requires haste.

If those of you who are unsaved only knew how simple it is to be prepared for these awful days which lie ahead and which are so graphically described in the Word of God, you would not put it off one moment longer. God says there are three things that you must recognize and do. We have called them the A.B.C.'s of salvation. First of all, "A"—acknowledge that you are a sinner before Him. Accept God's estimate and His description of your condition as He lays it down in the Word of God. Without any good or righteousness of your own, admit and acknowledge that you are a sinner and cannot save yourself. That is the "A" of salvation. "B" is believe God's Word. Believe on the Lord Jesus Christ. Believe that if you will turn to Him now He will save you, not by feeling nor emotion, not by works nor by your own righteousness, but just by believing and receiving Christ. "C"—confess Him with your mouth, for He has said, "If thou shalt confess with thy mouth the Lord Jesus and believe in thine heart that God hath raised Him from the dead, thou shalt be saved" (Romans 10:9). Do it now. It is later than you think.

CHAPTER TEN

The Sign of Russia

Reference has already been made in passing to the outstanding sign of Gog and Magog in the latter days. If we were to choose the three most outstanding signs of the coming of Christ, we would have no difficulty in placing the rise of modern Russia among those first three signs. The political restoration of the nation of Israel is the first sign; the rise of Russia and the world-wide preaching of the Gospel are the second and third signs. Because of the phenomenal rise of the northern confederacy, its prominent place in the "end-time" program and its definite indication of the return of the Lord, we devote four chapters of this book to a more detailed discussion of the significance of this unmistakable fulfillment of prophecy.

May I suggest, therefore, that if you wish to get the most out of these messages, you read first, very carefully and repeatedly, the 38th and 39th chapters in Ezekiel. You will be amazed at the clarity of God's revelation concerning Russia, How the Bible predicted over twenty-five hundred years ago the very things which are happening today. A great deal of additional light has been shed upon the most recent events and developments in the far east by the amazing record in these two chapters.

WHO ARE GOG AND MAGOG?

The nations described in Ezekiel 38 and 39 are called "Gog and Magog." The first question we shall answer is the question of the identity of Gog and Magog. Here is the record in Ezekiel 38:

> And the word of the Lord came unto me, saying, Son of man, set thy face against Gog, the land of Magog, the chief prince of Meshech and Tubal, and prophesy against him,
>
> And say, Thus saith the Lord God; Behold, I am against thee, O Gog, the chief prince of Meshech and Tubal:
>
> And I will turn thee back, and put hooks into thy jaws, and I will bring thee forth, and all thine army, horses and horsemen, all of them clothed with all sorts of armour, even a great company with bucklers and shields, all of them handling swords (Ezekiel 38:1-4).

There are five definite points mentioned by God in these chapters concerning Gog and Magog.

1. The meaning of the words, "Gog and Magog."
2. The regions from which she comes.
3. Her allies in this great struggle.
4. Her policy, aims and program.
5. The time of her rise.

THE MEANING OF THE NAME, GOG

From the earliest religious writings we find that Bible students have identified Gog as the end-time ruler, or the prince of Russia. Magog is the land of Gog, or the land of the prince of Russia. My pulpit commentary suggests this interpretation. The great scholar, Gesenius, makes Gog to be the ruler of Russia and Magog, the land of Russia. My Bible encyclopedia definitely identifies Gog and Magog as the farthermost northern nations dwelling in the regions of the Caucasus and the Volga. A more accurate translation, it is pointed out, for the expression, "Gog and Magog the chief prince of Meshech and Tubal," would be "Gog of the land Magog, the Prince of Hosh, Meshech and Tubal."

The word, "chief", is "Rosh" in the original, so that Gog is actually called the "Prince of Russia." Magog refers to the country of Russia. Gog is the prince of Russia of the last days. History further reveals that Magog (the second son of Japheth in Genesis 10:1-2) and his descendants migrated early to the north in the region now occupied by Russia. The two other names, Meshech and Tubal, apply to the two chief cities of Magog, namely Moscow and the ancient Tobolsk. This has been the consensus of Bible expositors' opinion from its very earliest days. Magog is Russia; Gog its ruler of the latter days.

ITS LOCATION

We come now to the second identification of Gog as the prince, and Magog as the land of Russia. The location from which Gog comes in Ezekiel 38 and 39, definitely describes Russia. It can apply to no other nation. Quoting just a few passages will make this clear. In Ezekiel 39:2 we read that God will "Cause thee to come up from the north parts, and will bring thee upon the mountains of Israel." In verse six of chapter 38, they are said to come from the north quarters. Again, in verse 15 we read, "And thou shalt come from thy place out of the north parts, thou, and many people with thee, all of them riding upon horses, a great company, and a mighty army" (Ezekiel 38:15).

Gog will, according to the Word of God, descend upon the land of Israel from the extreme north. Remember, in this connection, that directions in Scripture are always in relation to Israel and Palestine. North in the Bible is always "North of Palestine." South is "South of Palestine." So with East and with West. We now have two identification marks:

1. Gog means Russia.
2. He comes from the extreme north, in the region where Russia today is holding forth.

Its Allies

We come now to the third revelation in these chapters. Russia's allies are identified and called, "Persia, Ethiopia, Lybia, Gomer and Togarmah." The first to strike our attention is Persia. In 1932, only 19 years ago, Moscow signed a treaty with Persia, providing, in the event of war, free access of Russia through the land of Persia to the Middle East and to Palestine. In 1935, three years after this treaty, the name of Persia was changed to Iran, so prominent in the news today. The next nation mentioned is Ethiopia. This evidently does not refer to the African Ethiopia, for there was also an ancient Ethiopia, called in Scripture, "Cush." This land was located in the region of Babylon adjoining the land of Persia. This is most likely, in the light of recent events, the Ethiopia of Ezekiel 38.

The same is true of Libya, the third nation mentioned as being allied with Gog. The old name for Libya was "Phut," another ancient Bible land in the same geographical location as Persia and Ethiopia, to the south of Russia.

The next nation, Gomer, offers no difficulty, as practically all expositers agree that it has reference to Germany. The last nation mentioned is Togarmah, identified as the nations of central Asia, traditional enemies of Israel and closely allied to Russia throughout their history.

A few years ago this prophecy of Ezekiel seemed remote. Today we have seen these countries silently infiltrated and taken over by Russia, brought under the hammer and the sickle together with the other Slavic people to the north of Palestine. Ezekiel said twenty-five hundred years ago that these nations would comprise the great northern federation of Gog and Magog. We are today living in the very day of the fulfillment of these prophecies. The name, Gog, means Russia, the location identifies Russia, its allies are the nations today already under the sway, or almost so, of Russia. The evidence is most complete.

Russia's Policy

The fourth thing in these chapters which identifies Gog and Magog is the description given by Ezekiel of the policies and the program of Russia today. Ezekiel tells us about this in chapter 38:10, "Thus saith the Lord God; It shall also come to pass, that at the same time shall things come into thy mind, and thou shalt think an evil thought." The next verse goes on to tell what this evil thought of Russia would be. Here it is, astounding and arresting in the light of Russia's program in the past few years: "And thou shalt say, I will go up to the land of unwalled villages; I will go to them that are at rest, that dwell safely, all of them dwelling without walls, and having neither bars nor gates" (Ezekiel 38:11).

How easy it is to see Russia's policy in these words! Her program has been, and is, one of aggression against weak and defenseless nations. They are described as lands of unprotected villages, without walls and defenses. By subtle propaganda, by fifth column activities, false promises, propaganda, by intimidation and infiltration she will seek to overrun and overpower her weaker neighbors. This prophecy is utterly amazing in the light of recent years. Russia has taken over Poland, Czechoslovakia, Romania, Yugoslavia and a host of other smaller nations. More recently, she has overrun China, Korea and Indo-China. Still Russia marches on. We have already predicted that Russia would not be defeated in Korea or in Indo-China. Recent events have corroborated and borne out this statement. God has clearly foretold that Russia will meet her doom only in Palestine, when she meets the western alliance of nations under the leadership of the superman upon the mountains of Israel. That is the place where God says the defeat of Russia will take place. Watch Palestine and the Middle East, for God has spoken, and when God speaks, He carries out His program. We are, and dare to be, dogmatic about this fact, for we have the clear teaching of the Word of God in this matter. Russia's program of aggression, bit by bit, is running true to form according to prophecy. What a wonderful book, *the* Book, the Bible! Oh that men would turn to this Book for their information and guidance in dealing with the present Russian crisis. Thank God, we need not as Christians, with an open Bible before us, be in darkness concerning the outcome of the present crisis. So far, then, we have been able definitely to identify Gog as Russia, first, by the name which is given to it, second, by its geographic location, third, by its allies and fourth, by its policies and program.

THE TIME OF RUSSIA'S RISE

We call your attention to just one other positive identification given in the Word of God, namely the time when this rise of Russia will occur. First, we must notice the position of Ezekiel 38 and 39 in the Scriptures. The preceding chapter (Ezekiel 37), contains the prophecy of the valley of dry bones. It tells of Israel's restoration back into the land of Palestine. Chapter 40, the chapter which follows 38 and 39, describes Israel's Kingdom rest and blessing after the Second Coming of Christ. In Chapter 37 we see Israel returning to Palestine. In Chapter 40 we see Israel at rest in Palestine.

Amazingly enough, between these two chapters we have Russia's final attack upon Israel and her utter defeat.

In addition to this, the time is definitely stated by Ezekiel. In Ezekiel 38:8 we read, "After many days thou shalt be visited: in the *latter years* thou shalt come into the land that is brought back from the sword, and is gathered out of many people, against the mountains of Israel, which have been always waste."

Again, in verse 16, we read this, "And thou shalt come up

against my people of Israel, as a cloud to cover the land;
it shall be in the *latter days*, and I will bring thee against my
land."

In perfect harmony with this, verses 14 and 15 say,

> Therefore, son of man, prophesy and say unto Gog,
> Thus saith the Lord God; In that day when my people of
> Israel dwelleth safely, shalt thou not know it?
> And thou shalt come from thy place out of the north
> parts (Ezekiel 38:14, 15).

These quotations identify the time when Russia shall make
her attack upon Israel with absolute certainty. It will be
after Israel is back in the land of Palestine. Israel is already
in the land. It is following Israel's restoration that these things
shall come to pass, according to the Word of God.

As we shall see in the next chapter, this final battle described in Ezekiel 38 will not occur until after the Rapture of
the Church, during the Tribulation period. We therefore
have a right to look for the imminent return of our Lord
as the next event in the program of God with the nations.
The stage is all set, Israel is in the land, Russia is on the
march, the United Nations described in Ezekiel 38 are seeking
to organize, waiting only for one man, the superman of the
last days, to unite them against the king of the north. Before this superman, the son of perdition, can appear, the Son
of God will first come to take the Church of Jesus Christ to
Himself before the final battle. Who knows how near that
day may be?

Even so, come, Lord Jesus.

CHAPTER ELEVEN

Russia's Place in Prophecy

Magog has already been identified as the land of Russia, and Gog, as her end-time leader. God's description in Ezekiel 38 and 39 fits so perfectly with the rise of Russia in these latter days that the most skeptical mind must be convinced of the glory and the accuracy of His wonderful word. Oh, that our diplomats and leaders might turn fully to what God has to say concerning this Russian threat of today!

WHEN WILL THIS BATTLE TAKE PLACE?

We wish now to show you when this battle described in Ezekiel will take place according to the Word of God. It will be *after* Israel is re-gathered in her own land. In chapter 38 we read:

> Therefore, son of man, prophesy and say unto Gog, Thus saith the Lord GOD; In that day when my people of Israel dwelleth safely, shalt thou not know it?
>
> And thou shalt come from thy place out of the north parts, thou, and many people with thee, all of them riding upon horses, a great company, and a mighty army:
>
> And thou shalt come up against my people of Israel, as a cloud to cover the land; it shall be in the latter days, and I will bring thee against my land, that the heathen may know me, when I shall be sanctified in thee, O Gog, before their eyes (Ezekiel 38:14-16).

Two things are positively declared in these verses. First, Russia's defeat will only come when she swoops down upon the land of Palestine. Secondly, her defeat will be after Israel has returned to the land. Israel is already in the land as a nation, enjoying a precarious and temporary peace. So the stage is already set for Russia's ultimate thrust. How much farther she will go with her diversion moves in other countries, such as the Balkans, Korea, Indo-China, Western Europe and Nepal, before she strikes at her real target, Israel and the land of Palestine, we do not know. There seems little left to prevent her from striking at any time.

In a recent conference between our President and the Prime Minister of Britain, it was reported that they agreed that the defense of Western Europe was the all-important thing before our strength is sapped by secondary attempts to stop Russia in other theatres of war, such as Korea and Indo-China. How I wish that I could remind them that according to the Word of God, the real area of defense must be in the Middle East and the land of Israel. Over a dozen verses in these two chapters in Ezekiel alone tell us that the final battle with Russia must be fought over Palestine. Only there will it be decided.

THE TIME OF THE BATTLE

To return to the question of just when this battle will occur. We have already proved that it will be *after* Israel's return to the land. It will also be *before* Israel's final establishment in the land under the reign of their Messiah. We can, therefore, definitely fix the time of Russia's defeat somewhere between Israel's national political restoration (which has taken place in the last three years) and the Second Coming of Christ at the end of the Tribulation. By the Second Coming of Christ we mean His return at the close of the Day of the Lord and the Tribulation upon this earth. We know, also, that the Rapture will occur seven years before this event called the "Second Coming."

THE TRIBULATION

This brings us to the Tribulation period. Since the Church will be raptured before the Tribulation, Russia will not be finally defeated until after the Church of Jesus Christ has been caught away. Ezekiel gives us more than a hint that it will be in the Tribulation period. In Ezekiel 38 we read:

> And it shall come to pass at the same time when Gog shall come against the land of Israel, saith the Lord GOD, that my fury shall come up in my face.
>
> For in my jealousy and in the fire of my wrath have I spoken, Surely in that day there shall be a great shaking (earthquake) in the land of Israel;
>
> So that the fishes of the sea, and the fowls of the heaven, and the beasts of the field, and all creeping things that creep upon the earth, and all the men that are upon the face of the earth, shall shake at my presence, and the mountains shall be thrown down, and the steep places shall fall, and every wall shall fall to the ground.
>
> And I will plead against him with pestilence and with blood; and I will rain upon him, and upon his bands, and upon the many people that are with him, an overflowing rain, and great hailstones, fire, and brimstones (Ezekiel 38:18-20, 22).

This immediately suggests the Tribulation, and places the battle in the period called the "Day of the Lord." Compare this graphic description with other passages dealing with the Tribulation. In Revelation 6, describing this same period of time, we read:

> And I beheld when he had opened the sixth seal, and, lo, there was a great earthquake; and the sun became black as sackcloth of hair, and the moon became as blood;
>
> And the kings of the earth, and the great men, and the rich men, and the chief captains, and the mighty men, and every bondman, and every free man, hid themselves in the dens and in the rocks of the mountains (Revelation 6:12, 15).

This passage is so strikingly similar to Ezekiel's description that we have little difficulty in recognizing both to be in the

Tribulation period. There is another description of the Tribulation in Revelation 16:20-21:

> And every island fled away, and the mountains were not found.
> And there fell upon men a great hail out of heaven, every stone about the weight of a talent (120 pounds).

Passages might be multiplied by the score to show that Ezekiel places this battle in the middle of the Tribulation period.

THE RAPTURE FIRST

We digress here for a moment to sound a note of comfort and cheer to the believer. Before this great battle takes place, Jesus is coming to take the Church unto Himself. We shall witness this battle from our place with Him in heaven. We will not be here, according to the promises of the Word. We shall have our new, glorified bodies at that time and be with Him forever, and with our loved ones who have gone on before. We shall witness our King, guiding and directing His program for this earth, from a place of safety in heaven.

The description of this great earthquake, the sun and the moon dark, the mountains leveled and islands disappearing, with fire and brimstone falling from heaven, strongly suggests atomic explosions. I personally believe the terrific disturbances of nature described in these chapters, as well as in Isaiah 13, Revelation 6 and I Peter 3, will be the result of atomic explosions, probably set off by man himself. They fit the description so perfectly in the light of what we know today about atomic power. Thank God, we will not be here at that time, but we shall be with Him. The Word is very definite and clear on this. In Revelation 4:1-3 we have the Rapture occurring before the breaking of the seven seals. In Isaiah 26 the Rapture occurs before the day of vengeance of our God. In I Thessalonians 5, Paul, after telling of the awful judgment of the Tribulation days says, "For God hath not appointed us to wrath, (and a study of this passage reveals it is

the wrath of the Tribulation) but to obtain salvation by our
Lord Jesus Christ" (I Thessalonians 5:9).

Again, in Revelation 3, we read this:

> Because thou hast kept the word of my patience, I also
> will keep thee from the hour of temptation, which shall
> come upon all the world, to try them that dwell upon the
> earth.
>
> Behold, I come quickly: hold that fast which thou hast,
> that no man take thy crown (Revelation 3:10-11).

Again, in Luke 21:28, Jesus says, after His graphic description of the coming Tribulation during which the great battle
will occur (read Luke 21 in the light of this verse), "And
when these things (the things during the Tribulation described by Jesus) begin to come to pass, then look up, and lift
up your heads; for your redemption draweth nigh" (Luke
21:28).

In this same connection, Jesus says in Luke 21:36, "Watch
ye therefore, and pray always, that ye may be accounted
worthy to escape all these things that shall come to pass, (during the Tribulation described in Luke 21) and to stand before
the Son of man."

There are numerous other passages assuring the believer
that Jesus will come for us before that great and terrible
Day of the Lord. That is our only hope today! That is our
only comfort! That is our "blessed hope." Jesus is coming
again to call us out with all the dead in Christ, to take us
forever unto Himself. If I did not believe this with all of my
heart and soul and strength, I would sink in utter despair.
I think I should stop preaching a Bible which could not be
trusted and believed. Bless the Lord, His Word is true, and
only the believer has the answer to the problems of a dying
world and age. Rejoice, O Christian, lift up your head!
"For yet a little while, and He that shall come will ·come, and
will not tarry" (Hebrews 10:37).

What shall we say to those who are still without the Lord

Jesus Christ? Until you come to Him personally, and receive Him as your Saviour, no one can hold out a single ray of hope for you. There is no other answer for the world's ills and for your sin apart from the Lord Jesus Christ. According to the Word of God, things will not improve and get better, but will rapidly become worse, the nations preparing for war, till suddenly the Lord takes His own unto Himself. Then will break upon this earth the terrible Tribulation, with pestilence and with sorrow and famine and war, supernatural monstrosities from the pit swarming over the earth, hailstones weighing a hundred and twenty pounds falling upon men, until it culminates in the great battle of Ezekiel 38, and then, soon after that, the final battle of Armageddon.

If you are still unsaved, you cannot afford to wait that long. It may then already be too late. Death may overtake you, or the Lord may come. Once the Lord has taken out His Church, all hope for you will be past forever. Those who have never heard the Gospel may still repent and be saved after the Rapture, but for you who hear it now and reject it, the door will be shut, and you will have to pass through the judgment of that awful day, and then perish in the lake of fire forever. Think what it would mean if Jesus should come this week, or within the next day.

Do not put off the matter of believing and receiving Christ as your Saviour, for one of these days it will be all over. Trust Him now, before it is forever too late.

You say, "I want to be saved, but I don't know how." Let me tell you. Right where you are, bow your head and cry to God for mercy. Tell Him that you will, the best that you can (that's all that God expects), trust His Son, the Lord Jesus Christ. Believe on Him who died and rose to save you, and "Thou shalt be saved."

Believe on the Lord Jesus Christ and thou shalt be saved

CHAPTER TWELVE

Gog and Magog in Revelation

In the previous chapters on the Gog and Magog of Ezekiel 38 and 39, we have established the fact that Magog is the country of Russia, and Gog is its end-time ruler. Gog is the prince of Rosh. The verse is correctly translated, as many have pointed out, "The Prince of Rosh or Russia." The countries associated with her, Iran, Cush, Phut, Germany and Togarmah, are stated to be her allies in the end-time struggle. Russia's program, as described in Ezekiel, is a program of infiltration and propagandizing of weaker nations, and, if necessary, overwhelming them by brute military force. This, according to the Word of God, will continue until Russia attacks her ultimate goal, the land of Palestine and God's ancient people, Israel, when she will be finally defeated by a federation of western nations after the pattern of the present-day United Nations. Five-sixths of Russia's armies will be killed in this Palestinian battle. The remnant (only 16% of the original armies) will be driven back into the uttermost parts of Siberia.

RUSSIA'S ARMIES

Before taking up the question of the relation between the Gog of Ezekiel and the Gog mentioned in Revelation 20, we wish to point out a few details concerning Russia's armies, prophesied by Ezekiel over twenty-five hundred years ago. In Ezekiel 38:7, God is speaking to Russia, "Be thou prepared, and prepare for thyself, thou, and all thy company that are assembled unto thee, and be thou a guard unto them."

Notice carefully that last phrase. "Be thou (Russia) a guard unto them," that is, to the lesser nations associated with the Gog of Russia. Now the word, guard, is "Mishmar" in the original Hebrew. It comes from the root word "shamar," which means to "protect" or to "watch over" or to "save." Gog, then, in this verse, is said to assume the role of the protector and the savior of it allies, the countries which it has conquered. One cannot fail to see the present propaganda plans of Russia in all of this. By her fifth column activities and subtle infiltration, through her many occult front organizations throughout the world, Russia today has set herself up as the Savior of the world. She promises, to those who submit to her communistic slavery, protection and salvation from the terrible fate of being crushed and swallowed up by the so-called capitalistic and imperialistic war mongers of America and Great Britain. That has been Russia's slogan over and over again, to the point of nausea. We have heard it to the point of disgust from the lips of Vishinsky, Gromeka, Stalin and all the lesser puppets who only know how to repeat the master's voice. That is Russia's cry today, "We are the savior of the world. We will save you from the awful doom of the capitalistic imperialism of the Western war mongers."

God said this would happen way back in Ezekiel 38. Russia would win over the smaller trembling nations with her flimsy lie of protection against her enemies. How wonderful and true is the Word of God!

HORSES AND HORSEMEN

Another arresting revelation concerning Russia in this chapter is the description of her armies as being composed of a great host of cavalry men. Ezekiel mentions a great army of horses and horsemen in verse 4. In verse 15 we read again of these great numbers of cavalry divisions, "And thou shalt come from thy place out of the north parts, thou, and many people with thee, all of them riding upon horses."

Daniel, describing this great battle, tells us of the same thing in Daniel 11:40, "And at the time of the end shall the king of the south push at him: and the king of the north (Russia) shall come against him like a whirlwind, with chariots, and with horsemen, and with many ships."

Here Daniel tells of Russia's great tanks, horsemen and ships. It is already a well-known fact that Russia possesses an unbelievable number of the latest tanks and probably the greatest navy of submarine ships in all the world. Our interest, however, lies especially in the horses which are mentioned. Russia has always been known for its breeding of horses. In addition to her vast mechanical forces, she has an unknown host of horsemen today. It is well-known that, in the last war, Germany's mechanized forces were met and virtually overcome by mounted Russian Cossacks. The Cossacks of Russia's earlier days too, are well known to historians. To-day there is a revival of this mounted program. Russia has been breeding, we are told, and producing a new breed of horses far superior to any known before in endurance, in stamina and resistance, especially in the coldest of weather. The most recent statistics reveal that Russia owns some 70% of all the horses in the entire world today. In mountainous terrain where heavy artillery cannot go, horses are able to travel with ease. In the mountains of Israel the last battle of Russia will be fought by great cavalry divisions.

Recently, the newspapers came out with the information that one of our military leaders has been under severe criticism in Korea for allowing five thousand mounted communists to cross the Yalu river against our forces, without even being detected by our observers and reconnaissance planes. Very interesting, indeed, (even though it is tragic) in the light of God's Word.

We have gone into some of these details to show how infallibly accurate is this Word of God, and to urge you to study this Book if you ever would be abreast of the times

and know what is going to happen. Oh, that the leaders of
the nations would turn to God's Word to find God's program!
How I wish that someone who sees these truths could gain
the ear of those who are today seeking to guide our Ship of
State through the rocky shoals of a humanly unknown and
uncharted sea.

THE GOG OF REVELATION

We feel that we should devote a little time to the study of
the difference between the Gog and Magog of Ezekiel, and
the Gog and Magog of Revelation 20, for they are not in any
sense the same, nor do they come at the same time. The
Apostle John speaks of another Gog in Revelation 20:

> And when the thousand years are expired, Satan shall
> be loosed out of his prison,
>
> And shall go out to deceive the nations which are in
> the four quarters of the earth, Gog and Magog, to gather
> them together to battle: the number of whom is as the
> sand of the sea.
>
> And they went up on the breadth of the earth, and
> compassed the camp of the saints about, and the beloved
> city: and fire came down from God out of heaven, and
> devoured them.
>
> And the devil that deceived them was cast into the lake
> of fire and brimstone, where the beast and the false prophet
> are, and shall be tormented day and night for ever and
> ever (Rev. 20:7-10).

This passage contrasts clearly with the record of Gog and
Magog in Ezekiel, which we have been particularly studying.
Notice the striking differences between them:

First, the time of battle is entirely different in these two
instances. In Ezekiel, Gog comes against Palestine during the
Tribulation period. In Revelation the rebellion of Gog is
one thousand years later, after the Millennium.

Secondly, the Gog of Ezekiel comes from the north. In
Revelation, Gog's armies come from the four corners of the
earth.

Thirdly, since the word "Gog" means "prince," Russia's hordes in the Tribulation are led by the prince of Russia. In Revelation 20, the Gog or prince is Satan himself, the prince of this world.

Fourthly, in Ezekiel, Gog, or the prince of Russia, is against Israel and God is against Gog. In Revelation, it is Gog against God and the saints of God in Jerusalem.

Fifthly, the armies of Russia in Ezekiel fall upon the mountains of Israel, and the remnant of only one-sixth of them are driven back into the north parts (probably Siberia) and possibly become the neucleus of the deceived nations to be destroyed in Revelation after the Millennium. The armies in Ezekiel 38 are destroyed by the sword and it takes seven months to bury their bodies in the land of Palestine. However, in Revelation 20, Gog never gets a chance to join battle, but, before a single shot is fired, God intervenes and sends fire from heaven, and destroys them. They are plunged alive into their doom, the devil is cast into the lake of fire with the beast and false prophet. Then follows the last judgment at the Great White Throne, and all the wicked are cast finally into hell.

THE NEXT EVENT

It is quite clear, then, that Russia's road today leads directly to her defeat in the not-distant future in the land of Israel, by a mighty federation of nations, patterned after the present United Nations now struggling with this very problem. Russia will not be a member of this United Nations anymore in the Tribulation time, but will be entirely on her own. The federation of nations which God will use to destroy Russia will be under the leadership of the superman, the man of sin and the beast out of the sea of Revelation 13. Russia has declared war upon God. Since the Russian revolution of 1918 things have come thick and fast. It seems that we are now nearing the climax. Gog has set its face against Almighty

God, making it a crime to believe in God, forbidding the right of religious assemblies, substituting for God in the schools the philosophy of Marxism and anti-God propaganda. Mothers are forbidden to teach their children about Christ. Russia's ultimate purpose and aim is the destruction of all Christians and all of Israel from the face of the earth.

How long it will be until God steps in we cannot tell, but the indications are that this cannot continue much longer. God's next move will be the return of the Lord Jesus Christ. Then, the hour of the world's greatest judgment and trial will come without any warning and God Himself will take a hand in settling the affairs of the nations.

A careful study of the prophecy of Joel, which we recommend to you, will show you there are two great battles mentioned in Joel's prophecy, one in the second chapter, and one in the third. In chapter two we have the northern army coming down with its terrible destruction, only to meet defeat. In the third chapter of Joel we have another battle subsequent to this one in which all the nations of the world will be engaged.

These in turn will be judged by God Himself. From the picture it seems quite clear that God will permit a federation of nations, patterned after the United Nations, under the leadership of the man of sin, to destroy Russia. God Himself will later destroy this federation of nations because of their rejection of Him. As we see the nations lined up today, Russia and her allies against the rest of the world, we have a foreshadowing of that which is to come in the near future. How soon it will be no one knows, but we confidently believe that the coming of the Lord is drawing near.

CHAPTER THIRTEEN

The Revived Roman Empire

> Thus saith the Lord God; It shall also come to pass, that
> at the same time shall things come into thy mind, and
> thou shalt think an evil thought:
>
> And thou shalt say, I will go up to the land of unwalled
> villages; I will go to them that are at rest, that dwell
> safely, all of them dwelling without walls, and having
> neither bars nor gates,
>
> To take a spoil, and to take a prey; to turn thine hand
> upon the desolate places that are now inhabited, and upon
> the people that are gathered out of the nations, which
> have gotten cattle and goods, which dwell in the midst of
> the land.
>
> Sheba, and Dedan, and the merchants of Tarshish, with
> all the young lions thereof, shall say unto thee, Art thou
> come to take a spoil? hast thou gathered thy company to
> take a prey? to carry away silver and gold, to take away
> cattle and goods, to take a great spoil? (Ezekiel 38:10-13)

The Bible clearly foretells that Russia will, in the latter
days, seek to conquer and subjugate all the world to com-
munism and the ungodly anti-Christian, anti-God philosophy
of its founders. She will go far in her attempt, only to meet
utter defeat when she finally invades the land of Israel. When
that happens, she will meet her Waterloo.

In the Scripture above, God reveals the nations which will
oppose Russia in this battle and overcome her. We have
already seen the nations that will be aligned with her. In the
thirteenth verse of Ezekiel 38 we have the nations mentioned
which will be used of the Lord to defeat Russia. The
nations mentioned here are Sheba, Dedan and Tarshish.

When Russia marches down to Palestine about the middle of the Tribulation period, she will be met by a vast army led by the superman, the antichirst of the end time. He will lead a mighty host against Russia with the resultant destruction of Russia's hordes. At the end of this Tribulation period, God Himself will judge the antichrist and his mighty armies, whom God first used to destroy the northern army of Gog. Just as God used Nebuchadnezzar of Babylon to chasten and to punish Israel, and then destroyed Nebuchadnezzar himself afterwards, so God will use the man of sin, and his end-time army of federated nations to drive Russia out of Palestine. Then, in the battle of Armageddon, God will destroy this federation of nations, itself, gathered under the antichrist at the Second Coming of Jesus Christ at the close of the Tribulation period.

Order of Events

This, then, is the order of events, as given in the Bible. First, Israel must be back in the land as a nation. This has already occurred as recently as three years ago. Then, Russia will press her program of piece-meal aggression, swallowing defenseless countries, one after another, all the time having in mind the ultimate conquest of the Middle East and Palestine. Before this occurs, however, the Church will be raptured to be with her Lord in Heaven.

After the Church is gone, the antichrist will unite the western nations, now represented by the United Nations, and will weld them into a great federation which will establish Israel in the land, rebuild the temple and befriend the nation of Israel. It is then that Russia will sweep down upon Palestine only to be defeated by this united group of nations under the antichrist.

The antichrist will then reveal his own wicked designs. He will suddenly turn upon Israel, whom he had befriended before, and, after the defeat of Russia, set up the image of abomination in Jerusalem and seek to exterminate the seed of Jacob. If God would not intervene, he would succeed, but the Lord will take care of His own. We read in the Scriptures, "Except those days were shortened, no flesh would be saved, but for the elect's sake those days shall be shortened" (Matthew 24:22).

THE SHIPS OF TARSHISH

This pattern of things appears perfectly clear from the Scriptures, if one will give it careful study. We wish to call your attention especially to Ezekiel 38, verse 13. After Russia comes to take the spoil of Palestine and has subjected the defenseless countries to her communistic rule, she will be opposed by certain nations which will stand in her way. Here is the verse again: "Sheba and Dedan, and the merchants of Tarshish, with all the young lions thereof, shall say unto thee, Art thou come to take a spoil? hast thou gathered thy company to take a prey? to carry away silver and gold, to take away cattle and goods, to take a great spoil?" (Ezekiel 38:13)

We see from this verse that Russia's advances are protested by these armies and her motives questioned. These countries are called Dedan, Sheba, Tarshish and her young lions. Sheba, according to Bible expositors, were the Arabian tribes in the south of Arabia. Dedan refers to a people in the same area. From the context it seems evident that they are the African colonies which are associated with Tarshish in this last final battle. When we come to the name Tarshish we have little difficulty identifying many of the United Nations who will defeat Russia in that day.

THE BRITISH EMPIRE

The name Tarshish occurs about twenty times in the Scriptures. A careful study of these passages reveals some very interesting things. I have had a most enjoyable time looking up each one of these passages in its setting and in its context.

Some wonderful truths have been brought to light. I mention a number of them which point very definitely to one nation, and her allies.

1. The Jews spake of Tarshish as the uttermost land in their knowledge, the land which was farthest west from Palestine. In those days, of course, nothing was known of the western hemisphere and to the Jews in Palestine the land to the uttermost west could, therefore, mean only England and the British Isles.

2. We are further told that it was a merchant nation. Its pre-eminence lay in the fact that it was a nation of traders. Ezekiel speaks of the "merchants of Tarshish" in verse 13 of chapter 38. It is also mentioned in other passages of the Scripture, especially in Jeremiah 23, verses 1 to 14.

3. Tarshish was a maritime nation, its chief means of trading was by ships because of its island location. In II Chronicles 9:21, in II Chronicles 20:36, in Psalm 48:7, in Isaiah 2:16 and in Isaiah 23:6, as well as in Jonah, we have mention made of ships in connection with the country of Tarshish, so that the expression, "ships of Tarshish," has become proverbial. In this connection, remember that Britain has been the outstanding maritime nation of history. The slogan, "Britania rules the waves," is well known to all of us.

4. Tarshish is identified as an island nation. The Bible speaks of the "isles" beyond the sea. By this the Israelite understood the islands beyond the Mediterranean. The words, "the Sea" or "Great Sea," were the Hebrew expression for the Mediterranean Sea. The only isles which are found there are the British Isles. (See Jeremiah 25:22)

5. Tarshish is also a nation with many colonies. Notice Ezekiel's words very carefully. Ezekiel says in the verse which we quoted, "the merchants of Tarshish with all the young lions thereof." Tarshish has cubs, called young lions. We all know the familiar symbol of a lion as the indication of Britain.

We speak of the British lion, and the figure of the lion on her banners, too is well-known. We speak of the Lion of England, and know just exactly to what it refers.

This lion has cubs, according to Ezekiel. Britain's colonization has produced a litter of mighty cubs, the United States, Canada, Australia, New Zealand, Egypt (all Britain's English-speaking allies) and her colonies in Africa, represented by Sheba and Dedan. After diligent and exhaustive research there is not a shadow of doubt in my mind that Dedan, Sheba and Tarshish in Ezekiel 38 can be nothing else than the Western empires headed by Britain and her healthiest cub, the United States.

These countries, Britain, the United States, Canada, Australia and the other English-speaking nations, have always been the defenders of Israel, have always been kind to the Jews. Over and over again they have given them haven and protected them against their enemies, and defended them, even though in the handling of the Palestine problem many mistakes have been made for which God in turn will also judge these nations. We refer specifically to the terrible mistake of seeking to divide the land of Palestine between the Arabs and the Jews. Generally speaking, however, these Western nations are the ones who have befriended Israel. It is no surprise to find in Ezekiel 38 that it will be these nations who will contest and question Russia's attempt to take Palestine, and, under God, defeat Gog and Magog when they come down in the Tribulation period.

BRING IT UP-TO-DATE

In the light of all this prophecy, isn't it wonderful to see this Word of God unfolding before our very eyes? It is a well-known fact in military and diplomatic circles that the ultimate goal of Russia is Palestine and the Middle East. Her treaty with Iran, her clever overtures to Israel, are well known. God will use these Western nations, now represented by the

United Nations, to defeat Russia's purpose. I suggest that you read very carefully the record in Ezekiel 39 which tells us of the defeat, the burial and the result of this great Russian invasion.

ARMAGEDDON

This battle between the United Nations and Russia at the end time described in the Scriptures is not to be confused with the battle of Armageddon, which will occur later at the coming of Christ at the close of the Tribulation period. The battle in Ezekiel 38 is between the Russian and United Nations of the Tribulation period, Sheba, Dedan, Tarshish and her young lions. The battle of Armageddon is between these end-time federated nations and God Himself.

Neither must we confuse the present United Nations with the last great united federation of nations at Armageddon. Before the final battle occurs the Church will be raptured. All believers will be taken out to be with the Lord. There will not be a single Christian left upon the earth. It will then be a simple matter for the antichrist, the man of sin, to deceive the peoples who are left, take over the United Nations and begin his vicious program of deception. After being the instrument in God's hand to destroy Russia, he will himself be judged by God Almighty at Armageddon.

These things are happening right before our eyes. Israel is already in the land after twenty-five hundred years of dispersion. That alone is sufficient indication of the end of the age. Add to this the phenomenal rise of the king of the north, Gog and Magog, and the picture becomes still clearer. Then add to all this the formation of United Nations, headed up by the Lion of Tarshish and the United States, as the only apparent thing which is able to retard Russia, and the picture becomes clearer still. It all adds up to the fulfillment of God's Word, it fits like a glove on a hand, a shoe on a foot, like a key in a lock. Can anyone read the Bible, then look at the current events, and not see this truth clearly and plainly written? There seems only one thing which stands between the ultimate fulfillment of the rest of prophecy. That event is the return of Christ for His Church. Jesus Himself said, "And when these things begin to come to pass, then look up, and lift up your heads; for your redemption draweth nigh" (Luke 21:28).

The believer sees in all this the fulfillment of God's Holy Word, and the blessed hope of His return. Soon "He that shall come will come, and will not tarry."

Now we have tried to give you an outline of the events about to happen in the future, as given in the Word of God. We merely skimmed the surface. We trust that these few words will stimulate your study, however, that you too may be ready when the Lord comes.

CHAPTER FOURTEEN

The Days of Lot

When Jesus gave His marvelous discourse to the disciples on the Mount of Olives, He made reference to two (and only two) periods of time in Old Testament history, the flood of Noah and the destruction of Sodom and Gomorrha. In referring to both of these He said, "As it was, so shall it be." When the conditions prevailing in the antediluvian days were repeated, it would indicate the end of the age. We have discussed this aspect of the latter days in a previous volume (*Daniel*). We shall, therefore, limit our discussion here to the days of Sodom and of Gomorrah. Our Lord Jesus said in Luke 17,

> Likewise also as it was in the days of Lot; they did eat,. they drank, they bought, they sold, they planted, they builded;
>
> But the same day that Lot went out of Sodom it rained fire and brimstone from heaven, and destroyed them all.
>
> Even thus shall it be in the day when the Son of man is revealed (Luke 17:28-30).

To know, therefore, just exactly what Jesus meant, it is necessary to examine the record of the destruction of Sodom and Gomorrah as found in the Scriptures. This record is very brief but highly revealing as found in Genesis 19.

> And there came two angels to Sodom at even; and Lot sat in the gate of Sodom: and Lot seeing them rose up to meet them; and he bowed himself with his face toward the ground;
>
> And he said, Behold now, my lords, turn in, I pray

you, into your servant's house, and tarry all night, and wash
your feet, and ye shall rise up early, and go on your ways.

But before they lay down, the men of the city, even the
men of Sodom, compassed the house round, both old and
young, all the people from every quarter:

And they called unto Lot, and said unto him, Where
are the men which came in to thee this night? bring
them out unto us, that we may know them (Genesis
19:1-2, 4-5)

The name, Sodom, has for centuries and millenniums
been associated with one of the most debasing, violent and
most repulsive of all forms of immorality. The sin of sodomy
above all sins causes decent people to recoil in horror and
disgust. When one wishes to express the very superlative in
immorality and indecency, we compare it with Sodom and
Gomorrah, where the loathesome sin of sodomy reached its
height.

It is, therefore, remarkable that, when Jesus would give us
a picture of the corruptness of the age just preceding His
Second Coming, He compared it to the days of the flood
and of Sodom and Gomorrah. To the question of the disciples
concerning the signs of His coming again, and the end of the
age, Jesus replied,

And as it was in the days of Noe, so shall it be also
in the days of the Son of man.

They did eat, they drank, they married wives, they were
given in marriage, until the day that Noe entered into
the ark, and the flood came, and destroyed them all.

Likewise also as it was in the days of Lot; they did eat,
they drank, they bought, they sold, they planted, they
builded;

But the same day that Lot went out of Sodom it rained
fire and brimstone from heaven, and destroyed them all.

Even thus shall it be in the day when the Son of man is
revealed (Luke 17:26-30).

Striking Similarity

You will notice a striking similarity between the days of Noah and the days of Lot, a similarity so striking that it cannot possibly be mere coincidence. Jesus uses these two periods of history to show us the world conditions as they will exist once again just before the return of the Lord. He says in essence. "Watch the signs of the times, when world conditions described before the flood of Noah and the destruction of Sodom occur again, then know that the Second Coming of the Son is near, even at your doors."

No Excuse for Ignorance

There is, therefore, no excuse for ignorance concerning the time of Christ's return, with an open Bible before us. Jesus said, "As it was in the days of the flood, so shall it be in the days of the coming of the Son of man. As it was in the days of Lot, even thus shall it be in the day when the Son of man is revealed." To know the signs of Christ's soon return, therefore, we need only to study the Bible record of the flood and of Sodom, for Jesus said, "As it was, so shall it be. When all these things begin to come to pass, lift up your heads, for your redemption draweth nigh." The whole story of these days to which Jesus refers and calls our attention is given in a few short chapters in Genesis, a record so brief that it can be read, all of it, in about thirty minutes. This being so, I repeat, there is no excuse for ignorance or doubt as to the time of Christ's return. When the conditions in Noah's day and Lot's day are repeated, then we know the time for our Lord's return must be almost here, according to His own words.

Then and Now

That time is almost here, as we shall see from a study of conditions in Noah's days, and especially the days of the destruction of Sodom and Gomorrah. The similarity, the parallel between the description of the world in those days and the days we are living in now, is so striking that anyone with an open mind must be convinced. Notice some of the things recorded in the Word concerning those days and see that they are being repeated right now before our eyes.

Jesus says the days of Noah and of Lot were days of great abundance. They were eating and they were drinking. Now, of course, there is nothing wrong with eating and drinking. They are quite essential. The implication of Christ, however, is that they lived *only* for eating and for drinking. They were interested only in physical food and drink, and rejected the bread and water of Life. It was an age of appetite. It was an age of gluttony and bacchanalianism. It is strongly implied that drinking here refers to drunkenness. The age before the flood, therefore, was an age of appetite. They lived to eat and to drink. We have in the very fact that poor old Noah got drunk soon after the flood more than a hint of the influence this age left even on this saint of God after the flood.

We need not stretch the truth to call your attention to the fact that this description of the days of Noah (and the same is said of the days of Lot) fits this present generation like a glove. Today the average man and woman also live for appetite, gluttony and drunkenness, while rejecting the water of Life. It is estimated that in our gluttony we waste and throw away enough food to feed the starving people of the entire world. The consumption of intoxicating beverages and liquors in the United States has reached proportions never dreamed of before. Social drinking has become almost universal. Drunkenness has increased a thousand-fold. The liquor and beer business has assumed such proportions that the money spent for intoxicants alone would pay our national debt in only a few years. This tremendous cost is almost unthinkable. The cost in hospital and funeral bills as a result of drunken driving cannot, of course, be estimated, let alone the starving wives and babies of these men. Only eternity will reveal that legalized alcohol, not cancer, heart disease or tuberculosis, has been the greatest killer. We few believers cannot open our newspaper without being faced with men of "extinction" who have switched to some deadly poison or other. We can hardly tune in our radios anymore without some beer salesman berating us because we have not yet tried the superlative qualities of extra pale, extra dry, exhilarating, captivating, sensational, bla-bla beer. There ought to be a law protecting the folks who do not go for these things. I trust you will see the implication of Jesus, therefore, when He compared the last days to the days of Sodom. It was an age of satisfying the fleshly appetites.

AN AGE OF SEX

The second thing Jesus mentions as characterizing the days of Sodom is that it was an age of sex. Now there is nothing sinful or immoral in sex. Sex is neither moral nor immoral. It is a-moral. The morality or immorality of sex is determined by its use or abuse by the individual. The days of Noah and Lot were days of immoral sex abuse. This, too, the Lord Jesus Christ strongly implies in the words of Luke 17, and in Matthew 24 where He says "that they married wives and were given in marriage." The interpretation of Jesus is not that there is anything wrong in marriage itself. That would be a contradiction of God's own Word, Who said "It is not good for man to be alone." Our Lord, rather, implies the abuse of marriage. The word in the phrase, "they married wives," which should be especially emphasized, is that last word, "wives." It was an age of utter disregard for God's order of monogamy, one man and one wife. The Bible says, "Male and female, created He them," not male and several females.

The utter disregard for the sacred marriage relationship and giving way to immoral sex indulgence is the second sign of the age of Christ's return, which is all too evident today. How clear this becomes when we study the days of Noah and Sodom. In Genesis 4:19 we read "And Lamech took unto him two wives." This, by the way, is the first mention of polygamy in the Scriptures. It is recorded in the days before the flood, of which Jesus said, "As it was in the days of Noah, so also shall it be in the days of the coming of the Son of man." We need do little more than call your attention to its parallel in these days. In one generation we have witnessed the break-down of the home, the utter disregard of the sanctity of marriage, the terrible increase in juvenile delinquency with all of its immoral consequences. In forty years, from 1908 to 1948, divorce has increased from one divorce in forty marriages to one divorce in three, an increase of almost fourteen hundred percent! Today, as the days of Noah, is an age of sex.

True Also In Sodom

What was true in the days of Noah was still more true in the days of Lot. It too was an age of the grossest immorality. In Genesis 19, we find two men coming to visit the one believing family in the entire city of Sodom. Lot entertains them, and that night, we read this record:

> But before they lay down, the men of the city, even the men of Sodom, compassed the house round, both old and young, all the people from every quarter:
> And they called unto Lot, and said unto him, Where are the men which came in to thee this night? bring them out unto us, that we may know them (Gen. 19:4-5).

Here, then, is the first record of the sin of sodomy. Not only that, it was also the general practice of those days. What a shocking thing it is to read here, not only that the men of Sodom were guilty of this vile crime, but even the boys, for we read, "they compassed the house round, both old and young." It was this terrible sin which was the occasion for the destruction of the city, just as the immoral co-habitation of the sons of God with the daughters of men became the occasion for the flood in the days of Noah.

As It Was . . . So Shall It Be

Now remember that Jesus says, "As it was in the days of Lot, so shall it be in the days when the Son of man is revealed." Look about you and read your papers. Listen to your radios, read the government crime reports, send for information to the F.B.I. and remember the words of Jesus, "When those days are repeated, then the Lord will come in judgment."

A few weeks ago a man of forty-five was sentenced to six months to two years on a charge of gross immorality. The judge defended this severe penalty by stating he did it to set an example for the many juveniles who were guilty of this same thing in an established, organized way. Homosexuality among the employees of high position in the national government is so common that the authorities have been forced to make an investigation. Remember, it was this sin which was the occasion for Sodom's destruction and judgment. Jesus says, "As it was, so shall it be." How near the coming of the Lord must be! This cannot continue much longer. The flood could not come until Noah was safe in the ark. Sodom could not be destroyed until Lot was safely out. Since both of these incidents, according to Jesus, are pictures of the coming judgment, we know, too, that the judgment of the great Tribulation, will not and cannot come until God's people, His Church, has been taken safely out. The next thing, therefore, we believe with all our hearts, will be the Rapture when "the Lord Himself will descend from heaven with a shout, with the voice of the archangel, and with the trump of God: and the dead in Christ shall rise first: then we which are alive and remain shall be caught up together with them in clouds, to meet the Lord in the air" (I Thessalonians 4:16-17).

This is the blessed hope of the believer in a fast-dying age.

It is important that we recognize this fact that God did not bring the flood of Noah until Enoch had been raptured before the flood, and Noah had been made safe in the Ark. Noah and Enoch are typical of the spiritual believer who will be taken up at the coming of the Lord. It is a significant fact that Lot also must be delivered from the city before the judgment can fall upon it. There is a significant statement found in the 19th chapter of Genesis which records the escape of Lot,

> Haste thee, escape thither; for I cannot do any thing till thou be come thither. Therefore the name of the city was called Zoar.
>
> The sun was risen upon the earth when Lot entered into Zoar.
>
> Then the Lord rained upon Sodom and upon Gomorrah brimstone and fire from the Lord out of heaven (Genesis 19:22-24).

Note that God says He cannot do anything until Lot had escaped. Lot was a carnal believer. Yes! we find here that God is going to take out every believer. There will be a great difference at the judgment seat of Christ. Lot went out in shame and disgrace, while Noah went in faith and by the grace of God. We believe with all our hearts that the next event is this which is foreshadowed by the history of the flood and Sodom and Gomorrah. We believe that soon the Lord is going to come and we as believers will be taken out. Those who are ready will receive a reward, and go in to an abundant entrance. Those who have been living, fleshly, carnal lives will have to pass through the fires of the judgment seat of Christ and be purified before they are fit to reign with Christ in the Millennium.

CHAPTER FIFTEEN

The Age of Sex

> And as it was in the days of Noe, so shall it be also in the days of the Son of man.
>
> They did eat, they drank, they married wives, they were given in marriage, until the day that Noe entered into the ark, and the flood came, and destroyed them all.
>
> Likewise also as it was in the days of Lot; they did eat, they drank, they bought, they sold, they planted, they builded;
>
> But the same day that Lot went out of Sodom it rained fire and brimstone from heaven, and destroyed them all.
>
> Even thus shall it be in the day when the Son of man is revealed (Luke 17:26-30).

Jesus Christ is coming back again some day, to judge the nations and the world for their ungodliness and wickedness and disregard for God and His Word. This day of judgment is called in Scripture, the "day of the Lord," the "day of the Son of man," "the tribulation," the "day of vengeance of our God," "the time of Jacob's trouble" and many other highly-descriptive, colorful names. The description of this awful day of Judgment occupies a large part of Scripture revelation, in the Old as well as the New Testament. All one needs to do is to read the scores and scores of passages about the "day of the Lord" in the Old Testament. Jesus gave an elaborate description of this coming day in Matthew 24 and Luke 21. Almost the entire Book of the Revelation is occupied with a dramatic description of this terrible Tribulation day.

AT JESUS' COMING

This day of judgment, "the day of the Lord," will be ushered in at the Second Coming of Jesus Christ. There are two periods of history which, according to our Lord, are pictures, shadows of this coming terrible day. They are, first, the flood of Noah, and second, the destruction of the cities of Sodom and Gomorrah. When the disciples asked Jesus, "Tell us, what shall be the sign of thy coming and the end of the world?", He gave them a long list of signs, political, economic, moral, industrial and spiritual, which would announce the imminent coming of Christ and the Day of the Lord. He refers us to just two periods of history in which all of these things were also present. These two periods of history are the flood of Noah and the destruction of Sodom and the cities of the plain. Just before the return of our Lord and the judgment of the Tribulation period, the days of Noah and the days of Lot, according to Christ, will be repeated. Remember, "As it was in the days of Noah, and the days of Lot, so shall it be in the day of the coming of the Son of man." All we need to do, then, is to study the brief record of the days of Noah and of Lot, occupying less than a half-dozen chapters in the Bible, to find out what to look for just prior to Christ's return. When these days are being repeated, Jesus will come, according to His own promise.

THE DAYS ARE HERE NOW

The striking thing about all this is that the days of Noah and Lot are being repeated before our eyes. The days of Noah and Lot may be summed up under five primary headings, according to Christ.

1. It was an age of appetite. They were eating and drinking, the implication being that this was their main purpose in life.

2. It was an age of sex. They married and were given in

marriage. We shall see how true this was in the days of Noah, in the days of Lot and in the present day.

3. It was a day of commercialism. Jesus adds significantly, "They bought, they sold." It was, therefore, an age of big business, and of general trading.

4. It was an agricultural age. "They planted," says Jesus. It was an age of great agricultural surpluses. We shall say more on this in a moment.

5. It was a construction age, for Jesus says, "They builded."

These are the five things which Jesus mentions. We have but to turn to the Old Testament to find the record, and then to our newspapers, to see that it is the same thing again today. We may well call this the age of appetite, of sex, of commercialism, of agriculture, of building and construction.

SEE THE RECORD

When we turn to Genesis chapter 4, which records the history of man just prior to the flood, we find the record of this age to which our Lord Jesus Christ refers in Matthew 24 and Luke 17. Six things are mentioned in Genesis chapter 4:

1. It was an age of city building. In Genesis 4:17 we have the first record of the building of a city by Cain and his descendants.

2. It was an age of sex abuse, for we read in verse 19, "And Lamech took unto him two wives," the first record in Scripture, or in all of history, of polygamy.

3. It was an age of agriculture and of animal husbandry. In verse 20 we read that Jabal is the first cattle breeder of all history.

4. It was an age of culture and an age of music. Jubal, in verse 21, is the first musician ever mentioned in history or in the Scriptures.

5. It was, significantly, the industrial age, the age of metal. We read in Gen. 4:22 of Tubal-cain that he was an instructor in the artifice of brass and of iron.

6. Finally, it was an age of violence and boasting and pride, as we see in the case of Lamech who not only committed murder, but boasted about it openly.

This, in brief, is the record of mankind before the flood. Jesus says, "Even so shall it be also in the days of the coming of the Son of man." We marvel at the words of the Lord Jesus Christ when we recognize how accurately He describes the age in which we are living today in every detail.

Sodom and Gomorrah

The marvel increases and our wonderment grows when we turn from the days of Noah to the days of Lot. The record, indeed, is very brief, but packed with detail. Bear in mind the words of the Lord Jesus, "As it was in those days, so shall it be again."

The first mention of the conditions in Sodom and Gomorrah we find in Genesis 13. Lot chose to dwell in the beautiful plain of Sodom and we read God's own comment, "But the men of Sodom were wicked and sinners before the Lord exceedingly" (Gen. 13:13). It was an exceedingly sinful and wicked city. Sodom is a picture, according to the Lord Jesus Christ Himself, of the world just prior to His Second Coming.

The days of Lot were also days of warfare. Genesis 14 gives us the very first mention of organized war in all of history, either secular or sacred. The kings of the north swooped down and captured the cities of the plain, only to be delivered by Abraham and his army. How very significant. Here we have the first mention of warfare in the Bible, or in all of history. One of the first things which Jesus gave us as a sign of His coming again, was wars and rumors of wars.

We have already seen that it was an age of gross immorality. The very word, "sodomy" and "sodomite," which suggest the most loathesome of all immoral sex practices, find their origin in the word, "Sodom." You can read the sordid record in Genesis 19 for yourself. Sad to say, the sin of sodomy is the sin of today. Sex crimes, homosexuality, gruesome practices are recorded daily in our newspapers and reported over the radio. A generation ago they were quite rare, compared to the records of today. Organized clubs for the practice of the most lewd and loathesome crimes exist today. The matter of sex in itself, a holy gift of God for the perpetuation of the race, is the butt of public joking, wisecracks and gags. Sometimes it seems that programs are not considered "tops" without suggestive gags and filthy suggestions. The sad part is that these filthy comedians are responding to public demand. This sordid condition is not only caused by, but aids and abets the downward trend of morals today. Entertainments which emphasize the nude in the name of art, strip-teasing and the exploitation of the immodest, have all produced a condition of Sodom and surely portend a baptism of fire and judgment like the one that fell on that wicked city.

The trend in clothing, public appearances in shorts, our shocking bathing costumes, the perennial punning of gagsters about figures and "bras" and "girdles," is revolting and nauseating to the minds which still have a vestige of Christian decency left. People who want to be called cultured will applaud and support and encourage this form of vulgar entertainment. I am not talking now about the unspeakable rottenness of the dives and the honky-tonks and the night clubs, but of the things which are open and publicly practiced by the people who ought to know better.

Our magazines are an example of this very trend. I am not a sissy. I consider myself, a red-blooded he-man, but my modesty is outraged and I blush to be seen reading the average magazine with its advertisements featuring the suggestive, if not down-right immoral. Take our advertising today. Why can't we advertize a product, except against the background of a near-nude female? But why go on along this line? I trust you can see for yourself that the days of Sodom are being repeated before our eyes.

ALL AROUND US

The biggest problem of the F.B.I. today is the increase of sex crimes, especially among juveniles. News items list every conceivable type of sex crime, from indecent exposure to rape. The days of Sodom are being repeated today. Read Genesis 19 for yourself, with all of its sordid implications. Then pick up your newspaper and turn on your radio. The words of Jesus will begin to mean something to you.

DARK PICTURE

This, indeed, is a dark picture. We do not like to paint it, but we, as servants of the Lord, have no choice but to preach the truth as it is given in the Word of God. To the believer and the student of Scripture, it is no surprise at all that these things are occurring, for we have been warned sufficiently. Things are happening just as the Bible said they would. To the believer, this dark and cloudy picture has a silver lining, for Jesus Himself said, "When ye see all these things begin to come to pass, then lift up your heads, for your redemption draweth nigh." In this connection it is well to remember the words of the Apostle Paul. Writing concerning the latter days and what would occur toward the end of the age, he says in II Timothy 3,

> This know also, that in the last days perilous times shall come.
>
> For men shall be lovers of their own selves, covetous, boasters, proud, blasphemers, disobedient to parents, unthankful, unholy,
>
> Without natural affection, trucebreakers, false accusers, incontinent, fierce, despisers of those that are good,
>
> Traitors, heady, highminded, lovers of pleasures more than lovers of God;
>
> Having a form of godliness, but denying the power thereof: from such turn away.

For of this sort are they which creep into houses, and
lead captive silly women laden with sins, led away with
divers lusts,

Ever learning, and never able to come to the knowledge
of the truth (II Tim. 3:1-7).

Yes, the Lord Jesus Christ is coming again, and He has
given us sufficient warning, in the days of Noah and in the
days of Lot, so that we may recognize these conditions when
they finally come to pass. They are here today. The only
hope is "that blessed hope." The world today is once more in
the throes of a struggle, an international problem which defies all human solution. Man is seeking desperately to pull
himself out of the quagmire of impending destruction, but
the Bible says that the only hope is the return of the Lord
Jesus Christ, when the King shall come and set up His
millennial reign and

> Jesus shall reign wher'er the sun
> Doth its successive journeys run;
> His kingdom reach from shore to shore,
> 'Til moons shall wax and wane no more.

CHAPTER SIXTEEN

The Three Sins of Sodom

> Likewise also as it was in the days of Lot; they did eat,
> they drank, they bought, they sold, they planted, they
> builded;
> But the same day that Lot went out of Sodom it rained
> fire and brimstone from heaven, and destroyed them all.
> Even thus shall it be in the day when the Son of man is
> revealed (Luke 17:28-30).

It seems that whatever testimony Lot may have had in
Sodom went entirely unheeded. Life in Sodom went on much
as usual until sudden destruction fell upon it from heaven.
They did eat, they drank, they bought, they sold, they planted
and they builded. Thus shall it be in the days of the coming
of the Son of man. What was true of Lot's day was true of
Noah's day also. Noah's testimony was largely unheeded.
There was no great revival before the flood. There was no
great wholesale turning to God in Lot's day. There were
less than ten believers in the whole district of Sodom and
Gomorrah. In fact, there were only three, Lot and his two
daughters. Even so shall it be in the day when the Son of
Man is revealed. Today, again, the company of true, Bible-
believing, born-again Christians is pitiably small in comparison
to the host of unbelievers. It is only the presence of this little
minority which is holding back the Judgment of Almighty
God. As long as that little flock of true believers in the
Lord Jesus Christ is in the world, as long as true, born-again
believers are still here, that Day of the Lord and Judgment
cannot come. It was thus in Noah's day. Until Noah was safe

in the ark and Enoch had been taken out before the flood, it could not come. It was thus also in Lot's day. Until Lot was safely out, the fire of judgment from heaven could not fall upon Sodom and Gomorrah. Even thus shall it also be in the days of the coming of the Son of man.

The Church Rapture

Jesus said of believers: "Ye are the salt of the earth." Salt does not prevent corruption, it only delays the corruption and retards the ultimate ruin of the things which are salted by it. Even so, the presence of Noah retarded the coming of the flood, but it did not prevent it from ultimately coming just the same. The presence of Lot retarded and held back the destruction of Sodom, but it did not prevent it. God had promised that until Lot was safely out, He would not destroy the city of Sodom. He had promised that until Noah was safe, the flood would not come. While neither the flood nor the destruction of Sodom could come until Noah and Lot were safe, nevertheless the judgment of God did fall when finally they were taken out in safety. Noah is the type of the spiritual believer; Lot is the type of the carnal believer.

Even so shall it be in the days of the coming of Christ. The true Church in the world is the only thing which is preventing God's Judgment falling at this very moment. She is still the salt of the earth, retarding and holding back the Judgment of Almighty God. God promised Abraham that as long as there were ten righteous men in the city of Sodom, He would not destroy it, but the Day of the Lord will come, just as soon as the Church is gone, and one of these days:

> The Lord himself shall descend from heaven with a shout, with the voice of the archangel, and with the trump of God: and the dead in Christ shall rise first:
> Then we which are alive and remain shall be caught up together with them in the clouds, to meet the Lord in the air: and so shall we ever be with the Lord (I Thess. 4:16-17).

That is God's Word. The Judgment will fall, and there will be nothing at all in the world to keep it back, for Jesus Himself says in Luke 17:29, "But the same day that Lot went out of Sodom it rained fire and brimstone from heaven, and destroyed them all."

These words, "The same day," are significant. Life, apparently, went on quite normally up to the very day that Lot was taken out of the city. There was no warning to the unbeliever of the impending disaster which was determined upon the city, nothing to indicate that its coming was near. The same is said of the flood in verse 27, where Jesus says, "They did eat, they drank, they married wives, they were given in marriage, until the day that Noe entered into the ark, and the flood came" (Luke 17:27).

There is no indication that any warning was given to the unbeliever. The only warning was the Word of God and the signs which only the believers had heeded. Even so shall it also be in the days of the coming of the Son of man. It will come as a complete and sudden surprise for the unbelieving world, with not a single second of warning in order that they may have an opportunity of repenting. Paul says in I Thessalonians 5,

> But of the times and the seasons, brethren, ye have no need that I write unto you.
> For yourselves know perfectly that the day of the Lord so cometh as a thief in the night.
> For when they shall say, Peace and safety; then sudden destruction cometh upon them, as travail upon a woman with child; and they shall not escape (I Thessalonians 5:1-3).

Here is another significant thing. As soon as Lot was out, the judgment of Almighty God fell upon the cities of the plain. There was no delay of any kind. The same was true of the flood. We read, for instance, that the same day that Noah had gone in, the judgment of God fell upon the wicked earth. From this it is perfectly clear that there will be no time elapsing between the Rapture of the Church and the beginning of the Judgment of the Tribulation. Once the Church has been caught away, there is nothing in all the world which will prevent the Tribulation from starting immediately. The man of sin, the antichrist, will be revealed. When the salt is gone, the corruption will set in immediately and unopposed.

How Near Is This Event?

Do you realize how near the coming of the Lord must be, from this description our Saviour has given us? One of these days Jesus is coming again to take out every believer. He will shout from the air, and the dead in Christ shall rise, living believers will be changed and join them. Together, they will be caught up to meet the Lord in the air. A world without a single believer—not a single Christian left to testify! Every last one of them will be gone. We sincerely believe that this day is imminent and near at hand. There is no other hope left for mankind, or for the world. We as believers, however, may know the nearness of that day, for while it will take the world by surprise and come as a thief in the night to them, without any warning, it is not to be so for the believer. We do know the times and the seasons, according to I Thessalonians 5:1, and while we cannot and do not set the day we may know that it is near. This is very plain from this passage in I Thessalonians,

> But ye, brethren, are not in darkness, that that day should overtake you as a thief.
> Ye are all the children of light, and the children of the day: we are not of the night, nor of darkness.
> Therefore let us not sleep, as do others, but let us watch and be sober.
> For they that sleep sleep in the night; and they that be drunken are drunken in the night.
> But let us who are of the day, be sober, putting on the breastplate of faith and love; and for an helmet, the hope of salvation.

> For God hath not appointed us to wrath, but to obtain
> salvation by our Lord Jesus Christ (I Thessalonians 5:4-9).

Let me point out two things in these remarkable verses. First of all, the coming of the Lord will not be a surprise for the spiritual believer. Secondly, it will be his salvation from the Tribulation period. Paul is very definitely speaking here of the coming of Christ, and the judgment of the Tribulation immediately to follow. He says in verse six and again in verses 9 and 10,

> Therefore let us not sleep, as do others, but let us watch
> and be sober.
> For God hath not appointed us to wrath, but to obtain
> salvation by our Lord Jesus Christ.
> Who died for us, that, whether we wake or sleep, we
> should live together with him (I Thessalonians 5:6, 9, 10).

These words, if carefully studied, are clear concerning the teaching of the Lord Jesus Christ. Whether we wake or sleep, that is, whether we are dead or alive, at the coming of the Lord Jesus, about which He is talking, we shall be saved from the wrath to come. We shall be taken out before the day of God's wrath falls upon the world.

THREE GREAT SIGNS

The Bible contains scores and scores of signs which are given to us so that we might know that His coming is near. The Lord Jesus gives us a long list of them. Paul, John and James add many more. Jesus said, "Study the days of Lot before the destruction of Sodom, and you will have a picture of the days just before my return."

We have already studied some of them, and seen that it was, first of all, an age of appetite. Secondly, it was an age of sex abuse. It was an industrial and agricultural age. It was an age of gross immorality and wickedness. The prophet Ezekiel adds three more characteristics of the days of Lot. In Ezekiel 16, the prophet is pronouncing God's judgment upon Jerusalem. In the course of his prediction he makes a most remarkable observation concerning Sodom. It is a most striking passage. Speaking to Jerusalem he says,

> As I live, saith the Lord God, Sodom thy sister hath not done, she nor her daughters, as thou hast done, thou and thy daughters.
>
> Behold, this was the iniquity of thy sister Sodom, pride, fulness of bread, and abundance of idleness was in her and in her daughters (Ezekiel 16:48-49).

Here, indeed, is a revelation that should make us sit up and take notice. The text says that the iniquity of Sodom was,

1. Pride
2. Fulness of bread
3. Abundance of idleness

Three sins characterized Sodom, pride, fulness of bread and idleness. It was an age of self-sufficiency, first of all. They felt no need of God. It was an age of great abundance of food, fulness of bread. It was an age of great surpluses of food stocks and products. Thirdly it was described as an age of abundance of idleness, not an abundance of unemployment, but idleness. There is a great difference between the two.

Today's Application

Compare this description with the condition of our own land today. It is, indeed, an age of pride. Man, forgetting God in his mad pride feels no more need of Him. Right now we are faced with one of the greatest crises in history. In the middle of an atomic age man is still thinking of settling the problems of international friction by war. Experts have told us over and over again that another war may mean the end of civilization. Yet, in spite of this, man will settle his differences by the suicide tactics of an atomic war. Christians everywhere should get on their knees before God and pray for our leaders, for our President and all those in authority in this dark hour. They should ask God to call the nation to repentance, to return to God and put our trust in Him first of all, instead of armaments and weapons of war. If we as a nation would turn to God, no nation or combination of nations, could ever defeat us. Instead, however, it seems that man in his all-sufficient pride feels no need for God, but still relies on the arm of flesh.

Three sins of Sodom are given in our text in Ezekiel 16, pride, prosperity and production.

Today is also an age of abundance of bread. So great are our surpluses in this land that our government is spending billions to support the price of our over-supply of produce. News items in various magazines and papers inform us that the government has purchased dried potatoes and stored a surplus of some 76,000,000 pounds of dried eggs at a cost of $98,000,000. 15,000,000 pounds of these are stored in an old quarry in Kansas. Just to keep these eggs will cost the government $2,000,000 for refrigeration and $22,000 for electricity per year. In addition, $136,000 must be paid in salaries. Nobody wants to eat the eggs. 50,000,000 bushels of potatoes have been bought for the government at a cost of $500,000,000. The government has bought enough supplies of wheat to bake twelve loaves of bread for every man, woman and child in the world and enough corn to supply ample corn starch, syrup and oil to last the United States five years. The government has butter enough to make a birthday cake for every child under fifteen for the next ten years and enough cotton for fifty-four house dresses for every woman in the land. We have all this surplus while we are paying the highest prices in all of history. I bring out these facts only to show how true Jesus' words are, "As it was in the days of Lot, so shall it be in the days when the Son of man shall be revealed." In Lot's day there was an over-supply of bread, and it was called the sin of Sodom.

OVER-PRODUCTION

One other sin of Sodom is mentioned in Ezekiel 16:49. It is called "abundance of idleness." It does not say, "unemployment," but "idleness." This was undoubtedly the result of over-production. Man was able to produce more than he needed. Therefore, he could reduce his working hours and have occasion for more idleness and all the wickedness which accompanies the sin of idleness.

As it was then, said Jesus, it shall be again. It is with us to-day. A generation ago our fathers worked six days a week, and rested only one. Today man works four-and-a-half or five days a week at the most. He plays two days and never rests at all. When God gave the Law to Israel He said, "Six days shalt thou labor and do all thy work, but the seventh day is the sabbath of the Lord thy God, in it thou shalt do no work." Thousands and thousands of sermons have been preached on the last part of that command, "do not work on the sabbath day," but I have yet to hear the first sermon on the first part of that command, "Six days shalt thou labor." "Six days shalt thou labor; the seventh day thou shalt not labor." The law of the seventh day is negative, "do not work." The law of the six days is positive, "thou shalt work six days." Why place such emphasis on the seventh, rest, and totally ignore the six days of work?

CAUSE OF IDLENESS

Today, man is doing his best to get away from this. Work is considered a curse, and something to be avoided. First, men fought for a five-day week, then, a forty-hour week, and so on and on. This condition has been produced by the technological, mechanical age in which we live. The invention of more and more labor-saving machinery has made it possible for men to work only part time, and still over-produce. Whatever the cause, however, the fact is here. Man has so much leisure time each week that he seeks pleasure in recreation, fun and sin. He spends his idleness seeking ways to please the flesh, until we have become a generation of pleasure-mad people. Idleness always breeds trouble. Much of the immorality and the wickedness and sin can be traced to the idleness of man today.

Where is the home where the family spends an evening together? With our automobiles, our parks, our beaches, our houses of pleasure, recreation places, taverns, theaters, etc., the average parent is not home enough to know his own children. There is a resultant increase in juvenile delinquency. When this condition in the days of Sodom became acute, God came and poured out His judgment upon the cities of the plain. Our Lord Jesus Christ said, "So shall it be in the days of the coming of the Son of man."

CHAPTER SEVENTEEN

The Sin of the Angels

> For if God spared not the angels that sinned, but cast them down to hell, and delivered them into chains of darkness, to be reserved unto judgment;
>
> And spared not the old world, but saved Noah the eighth person, a preacher of righteousness, bringing in the flood upon the world of the ungodly;
>
> And turning the cities of Sodom and Gomorrha into ashes condemned them with an overthrow, making them an ensample unto those that after should live ungodly;
>
> And delivered just Lot, vexed with the filthy conversation of the wicked.
>
> (For that righteous man dwelling among them, in seeing and hearing, vexed his righteous soul from day to day with their unlawful deeds;)
>
> The Lord knoweth how to deliver the godly out of temptations, and to reserve the unjust unto the day of judgment to be punished (II Peter 2:4-9).

Among the angelic beings there are two main groups, unfallen angels and fallen angels, also called demons. There are different kinds of fallen angels or demons, some more vicious and wicked than others. Many demons are loose today in the world, while others, because of their viciousness, have been cast into "Tartarus" and are held in chains of darkness until the Judgment Day. Their sin was of such a nature that God would not permit them any longer upon the earth, lest all mankind be corrupted and destroyed. Who these ultra-filthy, vicious demons are is suggested by Peter in the 5th verse of II Peter 2, where he calls attention to the flood of Noah, associating these particular demons with the days of Noah, which Jesus tells us were a shadow of the days of the coming of the Son of man.

Then it is that Peter calls attention to Sodom and Gomorrah, of which Jesus also said, "Likewise as it was in the days of Lot, so shall it also be in the days when the Son of man shall be revealed." To understand, therefore, who these fallen angels are who have already been cast down to Tartarus (the Greek word here translated "hell" is "Tartarus" in the original), we have but to turn to the record of the flood in Genesis 6, and Sodom and Gomorrah in Genesis chapter 19. Referring to this record we read in Genesis 6:

> And it came to pass, when men began to multiply on the face of the earth, and daughters were born unto them,
> That the sons of God saw the daughters of men that they were fair; and they took them wives of all which they chose.
> There were giants in the earth in those days; and also after that, when the sons of God came in unto the daughters of men, and they bare children to them, the same became mighty men which were of old, men of renown (Genesis 6:1, 2, 4).

These sons of God were the fallen angels of that day. In an effort to corrupt humanity they co-habited with the daughters of men, with the result that there were born a race of people half human, half demon, called "giants." These were supernatural men, called "mighty men," men of wickedness and corruption. Now the word, "giants," as it appears in our English Bible, the corrupted offspring of this unholy union, is "nephellim" in the original Hebrew, and means "the fallen ones." The word "nephellim" comes from the Hebrew word, "naphal" which means "to fall."

The expression, "the sons of God," therefore, is used in Scripture to describe angels, both the fallen and the unfallen angels in the Old Testament. In the Book of Job, when the sons of God came to present themselves before the Lord,

Satan was also among them (Job 1:6 and Job 2:1). These angelic beings, called sons of God, were also present at the creation of the world, when "all the sons of God shouted for joy." It was a certain class or group of these fallen angels, apparently more vicious and wicked than their companions, who, under the leadership of Satan, occasioned the flood of Noah. By an unnatural, supernatural and wicked union with the daughters of men they corrupted mankind by causing to be born this race of giants, fallen ones, half demon, half human half natural and half supernatural. It is the only way that we can explain this reference in Genesis 6 to these monstrosities called giants and fallen ones.

To say that the sons of God in Genesis 6 were the godly descendants of Seth, and that the daughters of men were the wicked children of Cain is beset by too many difficulties. It would mean that all of Seth's children were sons, and that Cain's were all daughters, that Seth's offspring were believers and Cain's were all unbelievers. Moreover, it would never explain why the result of this union of believers and unbelievers should result in physical monstrosities called "giants," a thing which is absolutely contrary to the experience of nature.

Occasion for the Flood

The view we take makes no difference as far as the teaching of Christ is concerned however. It is not worth arguing about. The really important thing to remember is that this union of the sons of God and the daughters of men was a terrible sin. It became the last straw in the days of antediluvian wickedness and the occasion for the swift judgment of God in the flood. The wickedness and the violence of man, the corruption that was present in those days, caused God to send the flood. With all this, God was longsuffering and patient. He waited patiently in the days of Noah, according to Peter. When this terrible sin of the sons of God and the daughters of men began, the Lord would wait no longer. This sin became the occasion and the signal for the intervention of Almighty God in judgment. This is very clear in Genesis 6, verse 2, "The sons of God saw the daughters of men that they were fair; and they took them wives of all which they chose."

Immediately after comes this record, "And the Lord said, My spirit shall not always strive with man for that he also is flesh" (Genesis 6:3). Then we have the following record in verses 5 to 7:

> And God saw that the wickedness of man was great in the earth, and that every imagination of the thoughts of his heart was only evil continually.
>
> And it repented the Lord that he had made man on the earth, and it grieved him at his heart.
>
> And the Lord said, I will destroy man whom I have created from the face of the earth; both man, and beast, and the creeping thing, and the fowls of the air; for it repenteth me that I have made them (Genesis 6:5-7).

I trust you see from these quotations that the immediate occasion for the coming of the flood was the union of the sons of God and the daughters of men. The Lord Jesus says, "As it was in the days of Noah, so shall it also be in the days of the coming of the Son of man. They did eat, they drank, they married and were given in marriage." The reference to marriage in the days of Noah can mean only one thing, the mixed marriages and the debauchery of womanhood in Noah's day as described in this chapter. So too, says Jesus, shall it be in the latter days of His coming.

Peter's Commentary

The entire picture becomes still clearer when we study what the Apostle Peter had to say on the matter. In II Peter 2 we read as follows:

> For if God spared not the angels that sinned, but cast them down to hell, and delivered them into chains of darkness, to be reserved unto judgment;

> And spared not the old world, but saved Noah the
> eighth person, a preacher of righteousness, bringing in the
> flood upon the world of the ungodly (II Peter 2:4-5).

You will notice here that Peter refers to these sons of God
in Noah's day and tells us that they were angels. Because of
the awful nature of their sin, God has bound them in chains
of darkness and cast them down into hell. The word "hell" in
this passage is "Tartarus," a special place for the incarceration
of these specially wicked angels. The Apostle Jude tells us
further what the sin of these angels was and in what it con-
sisted. Here is Jude's comment on this same matter,

> And the angels which kept not their first estate, but left
> their own habitation, he hath reserved in everlasting chains
> under darkness unto the judgment of the great day
> (Jude 6).

In the following verse we are told exactly what was the
nature of the sin of these angels.

> Even as Sodom and Gomorrah, and the cities about them
> in like manner, giving themselves over to fornication, and
> going after strange flesh, are set forth for an example, suf-
> fering the vengeance of eternal fire (Jude 7).

What was the awful sin of these angels before the flood?
The identical sin of Sodom and Gomorrah, fornication and
going after strange flesh. It was the abuse of sex, the debauchery of womanhood, the disregard for the sanctity of the
home and the violation of the strict prohibition of the unequal
yoke, the union of believers and unbelievers. In the flood, and
in Sodom and Gomorrah, the occasion for the judgment of
God was the disappearance of the line of separation between
God's people and the world.

Jesus said that when this condition was repeated, it would
be the occasion and signal for His coming again. We are
living in those very days today! This past generation has seen
the most terrible and appalling corruption of the Christian
home. The truth of separation is too commonly disregarded.
As we stated before, divorce has risen in the past forty years

from one in forty, to one in three. Juvenile delinquency, the direct result of broken homes, has increased by leaps and bounds. Sex crimes and immoralities have swept over our communities like a flood. Marriage of believers and unbelievers is not only becoming common but countenanced by those who ought to know better, justified by sentimental Christians. One of the greatest disappointments of my ministry is this, that after preaching the evil of mixed marriage and the unequal yoke for twenty-five years with all the power I knew, to see these same people to whom I have preached and who have been told God's will, nevertheless disregarding all of that teaching and flying into the face of the clear teaching of God against mixed marriages, only to repent when it is too late. Another brood of poor, innocent children have been born only to see the home broken up, to be deprived of a peaceful home where father and mother are together. I repeat, therefore, for I do want my hands to be clean in this matter, Christian men and women, God strictly forbids marriage with unbelievers. You cannot expect God's blessing upon your home if you disregard His Word. God's Word is very clear:

> Be ye not unequally yoked together with unbelievers; for what fellowship hath righteousness with unrighteousness? and what communion hath light with darkness?
>
> And what concord hath Christ with Belial? or what part hath he that believeth with an infidel?
>
> And what agreement hath the temple of God with idols? for ye are the temple of the living God; as God hath said, I will dwell in them, and walk in them; and I will be their God, and they shall be my people.
>
> Wherefore come out from among them, and be ye separate, saith the Lord, and touch not the unclean thing; and I will receive you,
>
> And will be a Father unto you, and ye shall be my sons and daughters, saith the Lord Almighty (II Corinthians 6:14-18).

There is no escaping these words of the Lord through inspiration. Let me take you back, therefore, to II Peter and see what happened to Sodom and Gomorrah because of this sin. Here is the record:

> And turning the cities of Sodom and Gomorrha into
> ashes condemned them with an overthrow, making them
> an ensample unto those that after should live ungodly;
> And delivered just Lot, vexed with the filthy conversation
> of the wicked (II Peter 2:6-7).

Remember, "so also shall it be in the days of the coming of Christ." Maybe you will ask, "well, what shall we do about it? If this is the way it is going to be, and Jesus said it would happen, we cannot stop it, for if we did, then Jesus would be proved wrong when He said, 'so shall it be.'" Our Lord said that these days *would* come; they have been determined in the plan of God. It is all in His program for this age. All of this is true. Things will continue to grow worse and worse. The days of Noah and Lot will be and are being repeated according to the Word of God.

There is something that we as Christians can do, however, things we should do. We can at least pray for our loved ones; we can live a separated life; we can warn God's people to have no part in this world's program; we can warn our young folks against the sins of the flood and Sodom; we can pray for our authorities that God may move upon them, so that the awful wave of iniquity may be stemmed; we parents can give up many activities and pleasures of the world and devote ourselves to staying more at home with our children and setting them an example; we can make our homes pure and wholesome and clean and godly and spiritual, and then we can claim God's promise, "Train up a child in the way he should go, and when he is old, he will not depart from it."

We, too, can give our support to those agencies which seek to curb this evil menace in our days. We can pray for those servants of God who still dare to lift their voices against this evil. You can encourage those who are crying aloud, sparing not, sending out this warning across the world.

There is one more thing we can do. We can look up and pray for the coming of the Lord with John, and say, "Even so, come, Lord Jesus." He said, "As it was in the days of Noah, so shall it be in the days of the coming of the Son of Man."

Jesus Christ is coming again, and, when He comes, He comes to deliver His own first, then He will pour out His judgment on a wicked world. It was so in Noah's day. The flood did not come until Enoch was raptured. So too, before God pours out the vials of wrath upon this world, the Church first will be taken out in the Rapture.

It was so in the days of Lot. This is what Peter says:

> And delivered just Lot, vexed with the filthy conversation of the wicked.
>
> (For that righteous man dwelling among them, in seeing and hearing, vexed his righteous soul from day to day with their unlawful deeds;)
>
> The Lord knoweth how to deliver the godly out of temptations, and to reserve the unjust unto the day of judgment to be punished (II Peter 2:7-9).

Noah, a spiritual believer, was made safe before the judgment, but Lot also, the carnal, worldly, fleshly believer was also saved before the judgment that fell. That is the clear record, no matter how we may try to twist it around. Lot was a righteous man, a believer, but worldly and carnal. Lot *was* a believer. One would never suspect it from the Old Testament record, but here it is, just as plain as can be in the record of Peter, for "that righteous man," we read, "dwelling among them, in seeing and hearing, vexed his righteous soul from day to day with their unlawful deeds." All believers will be caught away at the Rapture, but what a difference. Enoch walked with God and went home to his reward peacefully. Lot walked in the world and was saved, yes, but how was he saved? He was saved by the very skin of his teeth; he lost everything but his life, and was brought to safety with the smell of fire and brimstone upon him—saved so as by fire.

There will be two kinds of people in the Rapture, also, spiritual and carnal. There will be those who will have an abundant entrance and those who will be ashamed at Christ's appearing, those who will receive a reward and His "well done," and those who like Lot will be saved so as by fire, to be purified in the fires of the judgment seat of Christ, and then to take the lowest place in the kingdom. Christian, are you ready? The coming of Christ will not be a happy event for all believers, as some think—only for the ones who are clean. To others it will mean Judgment, before they are ready to enter in. Our sins have been judged at Calvary, the matter of eternal punishment has been settled for every believer, but, let me warn you, that if we are not living the life we should here when Christ comes, there will be a judgment seat of Christ when we shall have to give an account of what we have done and how we have lived. It will not be a pleasant experience to see all our works burned up, and ourselves saved by the very skin of our teeth.

Here is just a word to the sinner. If the righteous scarcely be saved, where will the sinner and the ungodly appear? What will God do to you when that day comes, when He comes in His righteousness to judge the world and to make right that which has been wrong throughout the ages? Today the door is still open, and you can still flee to Him for salvation. "Believe on the Lord Jesus Christ, and thou shalt be saved and thy house."

CHAPTER EIGHTEEN

The Atomic Bomb

In our discussion of the "signs of the times" we come now to a subject which brings us close to the "end time." The discovery of the secret of the constitution of matter, as revealed by the splitting of the atom, is one of the greatest proofs of the inspiration of the Scriptures and the approaching end of the age. The scores of Scripture passages dealing with the convulsions of nature, the heavens aflame, the earth being burned up, were always believed by Bible-believing Christians. Many of these passages can now be clearly understood in the light of recent developments in the field of neuclear fission. The numerous passages in the Bible which men scoffed at a few years ago have been removed from the field of the fantastic and the impossible and the incredible. They are today admitted by all, as wholly possible and highly probable. One such passage is found in II Peter 3:9-13.

> The Lord is not slack concerning his promise, as some men count slackness; but is longsuffering to us-ward, not willing that any should perish, but that all should come to repentance.
>
> But the day of the Lord will come as a thief in the night; in the which the heavens shall pass away with a great noise, and the elements shall melt with fervent heat, the earth also and the works that are therein shall be burned up.
>
> Seeing then that all these things shall be dissolved, what manner of persons ought ye to be in all holy conversation and godliness,
>
> Looking for and hasting unto the coming of the day of

God, wherein the heavens being on fire shall be dissolved,
and the elements shall melt with fervent heat?
Nevertheless we, according to his promise, look for new
heavens and a new earth, wherein dwelleth righteousness
(II Peter 3:9-13).

These are the amazing words of Almighty God given by the
Holy Spirit through the Apostle Peter. These words are true
and faithful, spoken by God who cannot lie. A few years
ago this description of a future destruction by fire might have
seemed fantastic to some. Today, in the light of recent
discoveries, it is not only possible, but probable. Scientists
have warned us that man now is in possession of knowledge
concerning atomic and cosmic energy which may well result
in the destruction of this entire world.

THE ATOMIC AGE

This age will go down in the history of eternity as the
atomic age, the age in which man, by God's permission, has
solved the secret of the universe, and now has in his hands
a power by which, if God would permit it, completely to destroy
himself and the world. This secret is not ours alone, but is
also in the possession of our enemies. The power to destroy
the world is in the hands of wicked men. This, indeed, is a
sobering thought to contemplate. It seems that, with this
knowledge, men forever would shun war and outlaw the
ravages of war once and for all. It seems that in the light
of all we know now about atomic energy, men would realize
that our differences *must* be settled by peaceful means, or all
must be destroyed together. Such is the depravity of human
nature and such is the deception of Satan, however, that man
instead of seeking to avert war is pressing it with greater
abandon than ever before in all of history.

PETER'S TESTIMONY

According to Peter's words in the Scripture we read
man will not learn his lesson. According to the Word of

God, this world will not continue in its present form forever, for God plainly says that there is a day coming when "the heavens shall pass away with a great noise, the elements shall melt with fervent heat, the earth also and the works that are therein shall be burned up" (II Peter 3:10).

The word for earth in this verse is "ge," the word used, not for the world of men, but for the material earth, consisting of the soil and the physical elements. This, says God, is going to be burned up with everything in it. By studying the geological makeup of this earth, we shall show how plausible and logical and probable Peter's statement is.

The Atom

Before taking up in detail Peter's description of how this earth will be destroyed by fire, I want to give you a simple picture of the physical structure of the atom as we know it today. We shall not go into any great detail, as you can read all about it in your magazines and the voluminous literature of recent years on the subject, by men who understand these things infinitely better than I. You can get all the available information by spending just a little time in the public library. So we shall confine ourselves to the simplest outline of the composition of the atom.

Meaning of the Word

All matter is composed of atoms. Until 1910 it was believed the atom was the smallest unit of matter. The word, *A—tom,* means "nondivisible," from the prefix, "a," meaning "not" and "tom," which means "to divide." The word, *atom,* therefore, means that it is the smallest particle into which matter can be divided. In 1910 (only 40 years ago) a British physicist, Lord Rutherford, first advanced the view that the atom was not the smallest unit of matter, but the atom itself was composed of highly complicated parts, as wonderful and intricate as the universe itself. From this discovery, then, we date the discovery of the structure of the atom.

Its Size and Structure

Everything in creation consists of these minute atoms. Every one of the elements is composed of atoms. To get some idea of the size of an atom, consider these facts. One teaspoonful of matter contains *one million billion atoms*. Each atom consists of a neucleus or a core. This neucleus has two parts, two particles, called protons and neutrons. The neutron is electrically neutral and carries no electrical charge. The proton is electrically positive carrying a positive charge of electricity. The number of neutrons varies in different elements. Now this neucleus, the inner core of the atom itself, is about *one trillionth* of an inch in diameter. Revolving around this central neucleus or core are minute particles called electrons, carrying a negative electrical charge. These electrons, whirling around the central neucleus at great speed, are comparable to the planets in our solar system, revolving around our sun. The distances of the electrons from the neucleus in the atom are comparable to the distances of the planets, the Earth, Venus, Jupiter, Mars and all the other solar planets, from the sun. You can see that the atom is very little actual mass but mostly space between the individual electrons and the neucleus, charged with atomic energy.

Our Solar System

If you can visualize our solar system, you will have a greatly enlarged picture of an atom. In the center of our solar system is the sun. Around it, whirling through space, revolve all the planets in this system, of which our earth is only one. Now the earth, one of the planets nearest to the sun, is 93,000,000 miles from the sun. Most of the other planets are much farther away, billions of miles, some of them. These planets are held in their orbits and in their relation to the sun and to each other by forces analagous and comparable to atomic energy, probably the same forces which hold the atom together.

If you can visualize this solar system with its sun in the

center and, about it, the planets reaching out billions of miles into space, yet all revolving about the central sun, then you can visualize an atom by reducing this picture until you have a similar system, so small that you can place *one million billion* of them in a single teaspoon. The neucleus corresponds to the sun. The electrons correspond to the planets. That is, in the simplest terms, an atom. While the solar system differs in many ways from the atom, it nevertheless gives an intelligent picture of how an atom is constructed.

Atomic Energy

The forces which hold together each individual atom are called atomic energy or power. It is the most powerful force known to man. The forces which hold together an atom are one million times more powerful than the chemical forces which hold together oxygen and hydrogen in a molecule of water. The power which holds together a molecule of water in turn is a thousand times stronger than the elastic forces which hold together a bar of steel.

These figures are staggering. It is very difficult for us to comprehend these things, but they do explain the tremendous power which is released by a handful of matter when its energy is set free in an atomic bomb. Scientists tell us that the atomic forces in one single ounce of matter, when released, are equal to the power output of Boulder Dam for an entire month.

Splitting the Atom

It was discovered by scientists that this energy could be released by splitting the neucleus of the atom, thereby releasing its tremendous power. This is called "atomic fission" or "splitting of the atom." If a neutron is shot like a bullet into the neucleus of an atom, blowing it apart, the atomic energy is released, sending out, in turn, the neutrons of which it is composed, like so many other bullets. These, in turn, strike other atoms, causing them in turn to explode, which in turn emit more neutron bullets to strike other atoms, and so on and on, indefinitely. This is called a chain reaction, building up unbelievable energy as it is released by the countless billions of atoms until the heat and the explosion reaches the most destructive proportions ever known to man.

To illustrate this chain reaction we might use the method of sending out chain letters. One person starts a letter, sends it to ten different persons, each one of whom is requested to send it in turn to ten others and each of these to ten more, and so on, indefinitely. If you will take your pencil and paper you can figure out that by the time this has been repeated only ten times, it would mean ten billion letters. This is called a branched chain, and is just exactly what happens when an atomic bomb is exploded.

In the next chapter we shall discuss something of the awful destructive power that ensues when this released energy of the atom is used in the atomic bomb. Before we come to the close of this chapter, however, we would point you to the God of the atom. We hope that we have not wearied you by this somewhat technical discussion, for we felt that it was essential to know these simple basic facts, if you are to appreciate the many, many Scripture references to which we shall have occasion to refer you in the coming chapters dealing with this subject. Thousands of years ago the prophets and apostles wrote about the things which science has recently discovered. We could not clearly understand them before. Now, with the discovery of the atom, we see that these men foretold all of this beforehand. We stand amazed before the revelation of the Scriptures and its detailed information given thousands of years in the advance of science today.

God Is the Creator of the Atom

As we stand bewildered and amazed at the knowledge that we have gained about the universe, we ask ourselves, "Who made this atom? Where did it start? How did it begin?

Where did it come from? What intelligence was able to conceive and what power was able to create such an intricate thing as an atom?" Here, indeed, is something which evolution cannot explain, and has never, to my knowledge, even attempted to do.

God says that He Himself made the atom. In Genesis 1:1 we read, "In the beginning God created the heaven and the earth." In John 1 we read:

> In the beginning was the Word, and the Word was with God, and the Word was God.
>
> The same was in the beginning with God.
>
> All things were made by him; and without him was not any thing made that was made (John 1:1-3).

Almighty God Himself made the atom out of nothing but Himself to begin with. Since God Himself is the Creator of the atom, the One who conceived it and the One who made it, He Himself also is the only One who holds the protection against the atomic disasters which man now has within his own power. We know that today our only hope in this atomic age is casting ourselves entirely upon the mercy and the wisdom of God. With the atom in the hands of wicked men throughout the world, there is no hope in anything, except turning to Him, and acknowledging Him. He alone is our salvation. In the Chapters to follow we shall show some of the things which we may expect unless man does turn to God. Let us, therefore, bow before this Creator. Jesus Christ, the Great Creator, is the One who not only made the atom but who also made salvation possible. By His Word the heavens were made. That is why Peter says, "By the word of God the heavens were of old" (II Peter 3:5).

This Creator is coming back again. All of us will have to stand before Him to give an account of what we have done with the revelation that He has given to us. God grant that we may receive Him before it is forever too late.

CHAPTER NINETEEN

The Hell Bomb

> Fear, and the pit, and the snare, are upon thee, O inhabitant of the earth.
>
> And it shall come to pass, that he who fleeth from the noise of the fear shall fall into the pit; and he that cometh up out of the midst of the pit shall be taken in the snare: for the windows from on high are open, and the foundations of the earth do shake (Isaiah 24:17-18).

This is Isaiah's description of an awful day of fear and destruction which is to come upon the earth. As I read these verses, one phrase, made popular since the atomic age, came vividly to my mind, "No place to hide." Isaiah describes this scene, "No place to hide." It is the picture of utter confusion, with fire pouring upon men from heaven and the foundations of the earth shaking.

The one thing suggested by this description is an atomic explosion of such magnitude that it affects most of the earth and the world. The verses which follow make this even more clear and likely when we read:

> The earth is utterly broken down, the earth is clean dissolved, the earth is moved exceedingly.
>
> The earth shall reel to and fro like a drunkard, and shall be removed like a cottage; and the transgression thereof shall be heavy upon it; and it shall fall and not rise again (Isaiah 24:19-20).

We simply cannot dismiss these words lightly, for these are the inspired words of the living, infallible God. It is the picture of a tremendous convulsion of nature whereby the earth is rocked out of its orbit and caused to fly off at a tangent, presumably by some tremendous explosion.

As a result of this tremendous conflagration, the sun shall be darkened, the moon shall cease to give her light. Whatever the cause may be, it will result in the destruction of the great mass of the earth's inhabitants. This same chapter begins with a description of this awful coming day, "Behold, the Lord maketh the earth empty, and maketh it waste, and turneth it upside down, and scattereth abroad the inhabitants thereof" (Isaiah 24:1).

With our present knowledge of atomic energy this scene is not anymore in the realm of fantastic imagination, but an absolute possibility and a distinct probability. We have been warned again and again by the men who developed the atomic bomb, that we are now in possession of a power which is unlimited. It is possible that a chain reaction and explosion may result which man cannot stop, and which could go on until it disrupted the entire solar system:

Sun and Moon Darkened

Over and over again we are told in Scripture of a day in the future when the sun shall be darkened and the moon shall fail to give her light and the stars be disturbed in their courses. We call your attention to only a few of the many passages.

> Behold, the day of the Lord cometh, cruel both with wrath and fierce anger, to lay the land desolate: and he shall destroy the sinners thereof out of it.
>
> For the stars of heaven and the constellations thereof shall not give their light: the sun shall be darkened in his going forth, and the moon shall not cause her light to shine (Isaiah 13:9-10).

The Prophet Joel, describing the defeat of the northern army in the day of Tribulation, says, "The earth shall quake before them; the heavens shall tremble: the sun and the moon shall be dark, and the stars shall withdraw their shining" (Joel 2:10).

When Shall It Be?

It remains for the Lord Jesus Christ Himself, however, to tell us when this will take place. In Matthew 24:29 He says, "Immediately after the tribulation of those days shall the sun be darkened, and the moon shall not give her light, and the stars shall fall from heaven, and the powers of the heavens shall be shaken."

Mark records the same thing in the thirteenth chapter of his gospel,

But in those days, after that tribulation, the sun shall be darkened, and the moon shall not give her light,
And the stars of heaven shall fall, and the powers that are in heaven shall be shaken (Mark 13:24-25).

Many, many more passages might be quoted. The consistent testimony of Scripture cannot be ignored. The cause of this tremendous convulsion in heaven and in earth has been somewhat indefinite in days gone by, but we now know the answer when we consider what science has discovered about the composition of matter, of which the earth, the atmosphere and the planetary heavens are composed.

Atomic Energy

We have already pointed out the tremendous power of the atom. One pound of uranium equals in destructive power five million pounds of T.N.T., the most powerful explosive we knew until the discovery of atomic energy. There is sufficient atomic energy in an ordinary nickle to destroy a city as large as New York. All matter is energy and power. Imagine what would happen if a sufficient quantity of this atomic energy were released. The effect upon the earth and even upon the universe would be indescribable. In the light of these facts, do the descriptions given in Scripture about the stars falling, the earth reeling and dissolving, the sun and the moon darkened, still seem fantastic to you? They certainly do not to me.

The descriptions of the explosion of the earth in the day of God sound like the atomic explosions in Hiroshima and Nagasaki. Two of the most primitive atomic bombs were dropped on these cities. We are almost unable, still, to calculate the result. You are all familiar with the pictures of the vast mushroom cloud which blotted out the sun, the tremendous destruction so terrific that its effects circled the globe. Scientists here in the United States can detect when an atomic explosion takes place in Russia and on the other side of the world. These explosions are produced by a pound or two of matter releasing its atomic energy. What would happen if thousands of tons were set off? Yes, Isaiah, Ezekiel, Joel and Peter were thousands of years ahead of science in their description of the effects of that day of tremendous convulsion.

When Will It Occur?

Jesus tells us that this tremendous catastrophic event will occur after the Tribulation period in the Day of the Lord. The final explosion, resulting in the destruction of the world, will occur after the Millennium at the end of time. To get an idea of what man can do, let me remind you that when one bomb exploded over Hiroshima, between one thousand and fifteen hundred feet over the city, it completely destroyed four square miles of the city and leveled structures ten miles away. Sixty thousand were killed in a second. One hundred and fifty thousand more were casualties. Some forty thousand have since perished, making the death toll, we are told, upwards of one hunderd thousand. The bomb over Nagasaki was still more destructive. Those bombs were primitive bombs. Tremendous strides have today produced bombs so many times more powerful that nobody knows or even dares to think of it. With the old bomb, one bomber carrying one atomic bomb destroyed a whole city. Eighty-five of those primitive bombs could destroy every major city in the United States in a single raid. It is estimated that an enemy with less than one thousand bombers could wipe out the whole nation in a matter of hours. Remember that this estimate is on the basis of the old type, the primitive atomic bomb.

THE HYDROGEN BOMB

Today, we are told, the power of modern atomic bombs has multiplied a hundred, yea, a thousand fold. The "H" bomb is reported to be one thousand times more powerful than the uranium bomb. How far will God permit man to go before this thing is stopped? When an atomic war breaks out, God will have to step in, for, we are told, "except those days were shortened there should no flesh be saved." Everything indeed would perish.

In conclusion, I want to press home two things. First of all, the Bible teaches that this world will some day explode with a detonation which will darken the sun and jar the stars out of their courses. This world in its present form will not continue forever, but, according to the Word of God, a new heaven and a new earth will have to take its place. Before this happens the old world will have to be destroyed. The passages we quoted from the Scriptures and many more leave no doubt on this matter. This passage from II Peter alone is sufficient. Peter says,

> But the day of the Lord will come as a thief in the night; in the which the heavens shall pass away with a great noise, and the elements shall melt with fervent heat, the earth also and the works that are therein shall be burned up.
>
> Seeing then that all these things shall be dissolved, what manner of persons ought ye to be in all holy conversation and godliness,
>
> Looking for and hasting unto the coming of the day of God, wherein the heavens being on fire shall be dissolved, and the elements shall melt with fervent heat?
>
> Nevertheless we, according to his promise, look for new heavens and a new earth, wherein dwelleth righteousness.
>
> Wherefore, beloved, seeing that ye look for such things,

be diligent that ye may be found of him in peace, without spot, and blameless (II Peter 3:10-14).

For the first time in history we can now clearly understand the possibility and the probability of these statements of the Apostle Peter. It is a most amazing thing that almost two thousand years ago, Peter, an uneducated fisherman, was able to give us this clear, unmistakable picture of what would happen in the latter days, in the days in which we are living. It is the most wonderful evidence of the inspiration of the Word of God to be found anywhere. We are told that those who are the most active in developing atomic fission are the first to admit that this thing is a possibility, even as Peter describes it. God's children always believed those passages, but we were not able to understand them as we are now able to in the light of recent developments. Today it is much easier to understand and believe these matters.

My second concluding thought is this: there is only one defense against the atomic bomb. It is to become a believer in the Lord Jesus Christ, a true, born-again Christian, saved by grace and by the finished work of the Lord Jesus. If a bomb should be dropped by which you perished, it would only mean, if you are a Christian, that it would be for you the door into heaven immediately. For the unsaved, however, it would mean to perish in the awful heat of an atomic disaster, and then to be cast forever into the lake of fire itself "where the fire is never quenched, and where the worm never dieth."

Before the final conflagration of the earth comes, the Church will be raptured according to the promise of God. The believer will not be here when the heavens are aflame with atomic fire, the elements melted and the earth burned up. The Lord has promised to keep us from that day of Tribulation which shall come upon the whole earth. Only as we realize this can we understand Peter when he says,

> Seeing then that all these things shall be dissolved,
> what manner of persons ought ye to be in all holy con-
> versation and godliness,
>
> Looking for and hasting unto the coming of the day of
> God, wherein the heavens being on fire shall be dissolved,
> and the elements shall melt with fervent heat? (II Peter
> 3:11-12)

We ask ourselves, how could Peter say that he was looking
for such a day, and hasting unto the day of God, wherein all
these things should explode? The only answer is that Peter
must have known that he would not be here when it was to
occur. In the eerie gloom of an atomic age, what a peace it
is to know that Jesus Christ is coming soon, to take us out
and away, before the great and terrible Day of the Lord shall
come. Our Lord Jesus Christ Himself has told us in Luke
21:28, "And when these things begin to come to pass, then
look up, and lift up your heads; for your redemption draweth
nigh."

Again in verse 36 He says, "Watch ye therefore, and pray
always, that ye may be accounted worthy to escape all these
things that shall come to pass, and to stand before the Son
of man" (Luke 21:36).

CHAPTER TWENTY

No Place to Hide

> Proclaim ye this among the Gentiles; Prepare war, wake up the mighty men, let all the men of war draw near; let them come up:
> Beat your plowshares into swords, and your pruninghooks into spears: let the weak say, I am strong.
> Assemble yourselves, and come, all ye heathen, and gather yourselves together round about: thither cause thy mighty ones to come down, O Lord (Joel 3:9-11).

This is Jehovah God's call to war. The prophet Joel, prophesying concerning the final battle of the ages, the battle of Armageddon, is commanded by the Lord to tell the nations to arm to the teeth for the final struggle. This passage is not as well known as the contrasting passage, the call to disarmament, found in Isaiah 2:4. The Prophet Isaiah, speaking of the setting up of Christ's Kingdom and His reign of peace says, "And he (Christ) shall judge among the nations, and shall rebuke many people: and they shall beat their swords into plowshares, and their spears into pruninghooks; nation shall not lift up sword against nation, neither shall they learn war any more."

This is a call to disarmament and world peace when Jesus is King upon the earth. Just before this comes, there will be the greatest armament race in all of history, according to Scripture, as described by the Prophet Joel. It is a declaration of world emergency, a call to total atomic war, conversion of the whole industrial economy to war production. This passage is not as well known as the opposite one in Isaiah, so we re-

peat it again. This is what God says to the nations of the
end time:

> Prepare war, wake up the mighty men, let all the men of
> war draw near; let them come up:
> Beat your plowshares into swords, and your pruninghooks
> into spears: let the weak say, I am strong (Joel 3:9-10).

That prophecy is being fulfilled before our eyes. For the
past five years, we are told, 50% of Russia's total industrial
production has gone into weapons of war. Now we, and with
us our Allies, after a brief, uneasy peace of five years, have
again converted our industrial program to all-out mobilization.
An army of four million is being contemplated, controls and
curtailments are again upon us, as we turn our hand to
creating the greatest war machine of all history. In short,
Joel's words are being fulfilled now. "Beat your plowshares
(agricultural implements) into swords, and your pruning
hooks into spears."

THE LAST WAR

It may well be the beginning of the last two brief battles
before the setting up of the kingdom of our Lord and Saviour
Jesus Christ. We say "brief" because they will in all probability be ended by atomic warfare. First, the conflict between
the King of the North, Russia, and the United Nations of the
restored Roman Empire, will result in Russia's destruction.
Shortly after, the battle of Armageddon will take place. These
battles are described in Joel 2 and 3.

THE DAY OF THE LORD

This final battle, the battle of Amageddon, will be at the
end of the Day of the Lord, and at the coming again of the
Lord Jesus Christ. Joel, under inspiration, describes this battle

> Multitudes, multitudes in the valley of decision: for the
> day of the Lord is near in the valley of decision (Joel
> 3:14).

Now this valley of decision is located in Palestine. The

Scripture makes this plain. In the first two verses of the chapter, (Joel 3:1-2) we have this information:

> For, behold, in those days, and in that time when I shall bring again the captivity of Judah and Jerusalem,
>
> I will also gather all nations, and will bring them down into the valley of Jehoshaphat, and will plead with them there for my people and for my heritage Israel, whom they have scattered among the nations, and parted my land (Joel 3:1-2).

It will, then, be in the days when Judah has been delivered. The Jews are already back in the land of Palestine; Judah's captivity has already been brought back in part at least. There has been a political restoration of the ancient kingdom of Israel. It is then that the armies of all the nations, according to the Word of God, shall gather in the valley of Jehoshaphat, a great plain between the hills of Megiddo in the north central region of Palestine.

THE LORD COMES

This battle will be brief, as I noted before. The Lord will cause a great earthquake, the sun will be darkened and the powers of heaven will be shaken. We have already suggested the similarity of this and other like descriptions in the Bible to the explosion of the atomic bombs. It is the same as Isaiah describes in Isaiah 13:

> Therefore I will shake the heavens, and the earth shall remove out of her place, in the wrath of the Lord of hosts, and in the day of his fierce anger.
>
> And it shall be as the chased roe, and as a sheep that no man taketh up: they shall every man turn to his own people, and flee every one into his own land (Isaiah 13:13-14).

The Lord says that the heavens shall be shaken, the earth leave its orbit and fly off at a tangent. A few years ago this would have sounded improbable, impossible and fantastic. Today, with our knowledge of atomic energy, informed persons can no longer doubt these words.

No Place To Hide

In preceding chapters we have given a bare outline of the structure of the atom, the method of destruction by atomic energy and what lies ahead. In the remainder of this chapter we would like to discuss the question, "What means of protection and defense have we against atomic destruction today?" Though many solutions have been suggested, it is also frankly conceded and admitted, by those who know, that we do not have, and probably never will discover, an adequate defense against atomic weapons. In short, as far as man is concerned, there is "No place to hide."

Radar Screen

It has been suggested by some that we set up a complete radar screen around our country to warn us of attacking planes and to intercept them before they reach us. Our topmost scientists, however, warn us that this, after all, is no adequate protection. Bombs could be placed in the war heads of stratosphere rocket bombs; V-2 rockets travelling at 3500 miles per hour could be launched from ships at sea. The German V-4 (the so-called "Vergeltungs Waffe 4"), was designed to reach the United States from Czechoslovakia. Military men have discussed rockets that could be shot across the ocean and hit within a square mile of their target. Against such tactics radar would be utterly useless.

Moreover, the small size of the present "A-bomb" makes the use of planes almost unnecessary. A compact mine or time bomb could be smuggled into a country and driven into a city in a truck or automobile. Simpler still, an atomic bomb, dissembled into its various parts, could be carried in piece-meal, and assembled in a basement, an empty lot, or any other hiding place. Once assembled, its time-mechanism could be set to explode at any given moment. It need not even be in the center of the area to be destroyed, but could be some distance outside. No method of detection at a distance is yet known to man. Top men in the field of science predict that atomic war will be a "pushbutton" affair. We would not even be able to know who set it off, and, therefore, could not retaliate, not knowing who the aggressor was. Any small nation that had possession of the bomb could do these things.

Go Underground

Again, it has been suggested that we disperse our population to cities of 100,000 or less, and place our industries underground. However, it is estimated that the cost of dispersing our population alone would reach three hundred billion dollars. Going underground would cripple both efficiency and health. It simply would not be worthwhile living under those conditions. We might just as well perish right away in the atomic explosion.

Outlaw the Bomb

Another proposal, and the most plausible one, is to outlaw the use of the atomic bomb. This, too, has met with very little success in this age of deceit, deception and lies. Suppose that each nation would promise not to use the weapon, how are we to know their word would be kept? We have already learned that with some nations treaties and promises are made only to be broken. A deceitful, lying nation could take advantage of the honesty of other nations by waiting until they were atomically defenseless, and then strike with her own secretly-manufactured bombs.

Another proposal put forward is international control, an international body to inspect periodically each nation's resources, and keep an eye on the possibility of any other nation's manufacture of the bomb, contrary to international law. The very necessity of an international inspection body defeats its own purpose. If we must live in a world of suspicion where it is necessary for us to inspect other nations, and they must inspect us, there can be little hope. Distrust of one another would itself break down the whole scheme at its very source. So far, then, there is no adequate defense, no place to hide. The only human hope is to prevent man from ever using the bomb. Knowing what we do about the human heart of the unregenerate man, the record of history and the Word of God, this will never be until one thing happens, the coming of the Prince of Peace to take the reins of world government. He alone can solve the problem and He will when He comes to "rule the nations with a rod of iron." Until then,

> The nations will rage and the people imagine a vain thing.
> The kings of the earth set themselves, and the rulers take counsel together, against the Lord, and against his anointed, saying,
> Let us break their bands asunder, and cast away their cords from us.
> He that sitteth in the heavens shall laugh: the Lord shall hold them in derision.
> Then shall he speak unto them in his wrath, and vex them in his sore displeasure.
> Yet have I set my king upon my holy hill of Zion (Psalm 2:1-6).

This is the Word of God which says that the nations will rage and go to war until they acknowledge Him and God's King sits upon His Throne in Zion. Until then, these conditions must continue. God's admonition in these verses is:

> Be wise now therefore, O ye kings: be instructed ye judges of the earth.
> Serve the Lord with fear, and rejoice with trembling
> Kiss the Son, lest he be angry, and ye perish from the way (Psalm 2:10-12).

That is God's Word. This is God's only remedy, receiving the Lord Jesus Christ and acknowledging His Kingship. When He comes, then truly "every knee shall bow, . . . and every tongue confess that Jesus Christ is Lord to the glory of God the Father" (Phil. 2:11).

We have tried to give in these studies some simple facts about this awful instrument of destruction, the atomic bomb, in the light of prophecy. No escape for the sinner, but for the believer, a blessed hope. Before the final blast of judgment falls upon this earth, Jesus Christ is coming again. Our only defense against the coming Judgment, then, is to be a believer in Jesus Christ, to receive Him as our own personal Saviour. Then we are saved, and, thank God, we will be safe. It will matter little what may happen then. We believe the Prince of Peace is coming soon. The believer has these blessed promises written in the Blessed Book. How Satan would like to take it away! Even among fundamentalists there are those who would have us believe that we must go through this awful Tribulation period. How I do thank God that before that day comes, we have the promise that we shall be taken out.

CHAPTER TWENTY-ONE

The Mystery of the Ages

From the foregoing examinations of the signs of the times, it must by now be perfectly evident to the reader that we are rapidly nearing that event referred to by the Lord Jesus Christ when He said, "Even so shall it be in the days when the Son of man is revealed." The Lord Jesus Christ is surely coming again. This is an incontrovertible fact. We cannot know the day nor the hour. We do know, and should know, the "times and the seasons." When the Lord Jesus Christ ascended into heaven, He told His disciples, "It is not for you to know the times or the seasons, which the Father hath put in his own power" (Acts 1:7).

But, in Thessalonians Paul says this:

> But of the times and the seasons, brethren, ye have no need that I write unto you.
>
> For yourselves know perfectly that the day of the Lord so cometh as a thief in the night.
>
> For when they shall say, Peace and safety; then sudden destruction cometh upon them, as travail upon a woman with child; and they shall not escape (I Thessalonians 5:1-3).

Our Lord Jesus Christ said: "It is not for you to know the times nor the seasons." The Apostle Paul, writing many years afterward, told us that we may know the times and the seasons of the Lord's return. Now all of this sounds like a contradiction and a paradox, but it is nothing of the kind. Jesus spake *before* Pentecost. Paul spake *after* the Day of Pentecost. The mysteries of this age were not fully revealed until the

Holy Spirit came on the Day of Pentecost. Therefore, the disciples were not to know the times or the seasons until they should be revealed. It was only after the event of Pentecost that the mysteries of the kingdom were fully revealed through Paul and the Apostles. For that very reason Paul says in I Corinthians,

> Behold, I shew you a mystery: We shall not all sleep, but we shall all be changed,
>
> In a moment, in the twinkling of an eye, at the last trump; for the trumpet shall sound, and the dead shall be raised incorruptible, and we shall be changed.
>
> For this corruptible must put on incorruption, and this mortal must put on immortality.
>
> So when this corruptible shall have put on incorruption, and this mortal shall have put on immortality, then shall be brought to pass the saying that is written, Death is swallowed up in victory.
>
> O death, where is thy sting? O grave, where is thy victory?
>
> The sting of death is sin; but the strength of sin is the law.
>
> But thanks be unto God, which giveth us the victory through our Lord Jesus Christ (I Corinthians 15:51-57).

The most dramatic and wonderful event since the coming of Jesus Christ to Bethlehem is going to take place one of these days. This dramatic event will be the sudden exodus, by air, of millions of persons, the departure, simultaneously and instantaneously, of countless millions from this world, through the air, past the clouds, to meet their Saviour and their Lord.

This mass exodus of the saints we call the Rapture of the Church of Jesus Christ. While the exact word "Rapture" does not occur in our English Bible, the fact is clearly taught. It is called "translation" in Hebrews 11. It is called "caught up together" in I Thessalonians 4. This glorious event, when Jesus comes again to raise all the believing dead, change all the living believers and catch them all up to Himself, is called in Scripture, "that blessed hope." This event will occur sometime; it may occur anytime. Jesus said in John 14: "If I go away, I will also come again." We are nearer that event than we have ever been before in the history of the Church. We have never been as near the return of Christ as we are right now, at this very moment. One of these days it will happen, and

> The Lord Himself shall descend from heaven with a shout, with the voice of the archangel, and with the trump of God: and the dead in Christ shall rise first:
>
> Then we which are alive and remain shall be caught up together with them in the clouds, to meet the Lord in the air: and so shall we ever be with the Lord (I Thessalonians 4:16-17).

THE GREAT MYSTERY

This event, this "blessed hope," the resurrection of the dead and the translation of all believers in a single moment, is called by Paul in our Scripture a "mystery." He says, "Behold I shew you a *mystery*."

This event *is* a mystery in many different ways. It was a mystery to the Old Testament saints, since the full revelation of both the Church and her Rapture at Jesus' coming was never clearly revealed until after Pentecost. It is a mystery in another way. When this event occurs, it will be so sudden, so secret, that the unsaved who remain will be utterly confused, non-plussed and mystified by the unexplainable, sudden, dramatic disappearance of millions upon millions of believers without leaving a single trace or clue as to the method or the destination of their sudden departure.

BEHOLD, A MYSTERY!

This revelation of the Rapture is also a mystery *now* to the unbeliever. The unregenerate man does not understand or believe it. To him it is foolishness and the empty, will-o-the-wisp dream and hope of "other-worldly" Christians.

Peter predicted this when he said in II Peter,

> Knowing this first, that there shall come in the last
> days scoffers, walking after their own lusts,
>
> And saying. Where is the promise of his coming? for
> since our fathers fell asleep, all things continue as they
> were from the beginning of the creation (II Peter 3:3-4).

MEANING OF THE WORD

"Behold, I shew you a mystery!" The word translated
"mystery" is an interesting one. In the original Greek the
word is "mysterion." It comes from a root word "muo" which
means to "keep secret." Paul says, "Behold I shew you a
'deep secret.'" The word originally came from the practice
of ancient secret societies and was applied to their secret
pass-word and rituals. Only those who knew the "mysterion,"
the "secret pass-word," could enter and know the inner secrets
of the lodge, or secret order. This is the word Paul uses when
he says, "Behold, I shew you a mystery (or 'secret password')."
The truth of the Rapture is only for those who belong to that
body of believers who have been initiated into the inner sanc-
tum of the company of God's elect by faith in Jesus Christ
their Saviour. To all others these truths must remain a
mystery and of no concern.

Again, it is a mystery because only those who know the
password, only those who have been born again and washed
in the blood, will hear the shout when it occurs. When Jesus
comes and shouts from the air and the dead are raised and
living believers changed, only the saved will respond and will
understand the shout and rise to meet their Lord in the air.
The rest of the inhabitants of the earth may realize that
something has happened, but they will not know what it was.
It will be to them a mystery. When Paul was converted on
the way to Damascus a Voice spake to Paul and he understood
it. Not so with the rest who were with him. Paul tells us in
Acts 22:9, "And they that were with me saw indeed the

light, and were afraid; but they heard not the voice of him
that spake to me."

So, too, will it be in the day when Jesus calls the Church
unto Himself. Only believers will hear and understand His
voice and His call. If this seems strange to you, let me remind
you that while you listen to your radio you have a perfect
illustration of the fact that, when Jesus shouts, only certain
ones will be able to hear it and others will be ignorant of anything happening at all.

As I speak over the air, people hear my voice coming
through the loud-speaker, as clearly as though I were in the
same room. A neighbor next door does not hear a word that
I say. He doesn't even know that I am speaking. Why
not? Because he is not tuned in on the wave-length over
which I am talking. He has a radio, the same ether waves
which carry my voice through your set are passing through his
room. His set is turned on also, but he doesn't hear a word
of what I am saying, just because he is not tuned in to the
right wave-length.

STATION B-L-O-O-D

Just so it will be at the Rapture. Jesus will shout from
the air, but only the ones who are tuned in on station
F-A-I-T-H and B-L-O-O-D will be able to get the message. The
rest will hear nothing at all, while we who hear will be
instantaneously changed and rise to meet our Lord in the
air. As a magnet picks up only the steel and leaves the dross
behind, so only the Church, magnetized by the Spirit of God
and born again, will respond to His call. As the thief takes
only the jewelry, money and valuable articles and leaves the
rest undisturbed, so, too, it will be at the Rapture.

"Behold, I shew you a mystery." The dead *in christ* shall
rise first. Then living believers shall be changed. The apostle
Paul says we shall not *all* sleep. There will be one generation
of believers alive when Jesus comes who will never have to
pass through the experience of death. Paul is speaking of the

sleep of death when he says, we shall not *all* sleep." In the fifteenth chapter of I Corinthians, Paul had been dealing with the resurrection of the bodies of dead believers. He first discusses the resurrection of the Body of the Lord Jesus Christ, then the certainty of our own resurrection, then the nature of these resurrection bodies, then the order of this resurrection— "Christ the firstfruits, afterwards they that are Christ's at His coming."

In the passage which we quoted He says, "Behold, I shew you a mystery." The FACT of the resurrection was well known before this, but here comes something new which is called a "mystery." This is the mystery which Paul would have us to know. Some will never have to die. We (speaking of all believers in every age) shall not *all* sleep. The believers living when Jesus comes will never have to die. Those who have died will be raised incorruptible. This then is the mystery. This is "that blessed hope." This is the most thrilling, heart-warming comfort in the terrible days of darkness in which we are living today.

Jesus Is Coming Again

Yes, indeed, the Lord Jesus Christ is coming again. I wonder whether believers realize as they ought what this will mean to them. Jesus, at that time will bring our loved ones who have died in the faith with Him. We shall be reunited with them, never to part again. Those of us who are alive at that time will never have to die, but will instantaneously and painlessly be changed and raptured with all our saved loved ones, to be with Him and with them forevermore.

Personally, I do not care to die. The thought of death holds no comfort for me. I would rather not have to part with my loved ones, yet the only thing that will prevent this parting is the return of our blessed Lord Jesus. Parting with our precious loved ones is a heart-rending thing and all of us shrink naturally from it.

I trust that you will be able to see now why the Holy

Spirit Himself calls this event "that blessed hope." It means that when He comes you will meet your husband again, your wife who has gone before you, your mother. We shall be caught up together to meet the Lord in the air. "Behold, I shew you a mystery."

We must remember that it is only for believers. The lost will remain to face the wrath of Almighty God, to be separated from God and their loved ones forever and ever. I trust that these words will fix your eyes upon the glorious, future day which may be much nearer than we think, when our saved loved ones shall return with the Lord Jesus Christ and we, united with them, shall enter into His presence, never, never to part again. This is the only hope in the hour of sorrow, and it is no wonder that Paul admonished the Thessalonian Christians in their bereavement to "comfort one another with these words."

CHAPTER TWENTY-TWO

The Order of Christ's Coming

> Behold, I shew you a mystery; We shall not all sleep,
> but we shall all be changed,
> > In a moment, in the twinkling of an eye . . .
> (I Corinthians 15:51-52).

The age which began on the Day of Pentecost is an age of deep mystery. When Jesus came the first time nineteen hundred years ago, His people, Israel, knew nothing of this present age in which we live, the dispensation of the Church of Jesus Christ. They believed that, when their Messiah came, He would deliver them from their Gentile-Roman bondage and immediately set up the glorious Messianic-Israelitish kingdom which had been the theme and the hope of all the prophets before them.

This was the hope of His disciples also, who, time and again, came to Him and asked Him when He would inaugurate His kingdom and deliver Israel. They even disputed among themselves which ones would hold the most desirable seats in the King's cabinet. Even John the Baptist knew nothing of this present Church age, but saw only the Messianic kingdom. When he was cast into prison he sent to inquire of Jesus, "Art thou he that should come, or seek we for another?"

Even at the Ascension of the Lord Jesus Christ the disciples were still looking for the immediate setting up of the kingdom of the Messiah. They evidently believed that He had led them to Mount Olivet for the purpose of launching His campaign from that point, and so they inquired, "Wilt thou at this time restore again the kingdom to Israel?" (Acts 1:6) To that question Jesus answered, "It is not for you to know the times or the seasons, which the Father hath put in his own power" (Acts 1:7).

Instead of launching His kingdom to set up the Messianic rule of Israel, He left them, and went into heaven. He was suddenly taken up out of their sight into the blue. They were stunned; they were mystified; they were disappointed. They were completely frustrated, for all their fondest hopes were now dashed to the ground in a moment. But not for long, for Jesus sent two men right back from heaven with this message: "Ye men of Galilee, why stand ye gazing up into heaven? this same Jesus, which is taken up from you into heaven, shall so come in like manner as ye have seen him go into heaven" (Acts 1:11).

Here, then, was their comfort—Jesus was coming back again. What about the kingdom? What will happen in the meantime? What about all the promises made by the prophets in the Old Testament concerning the setting up of the Messianic kingdom upon the earth? Had they been misinformed about a literal kingdom on earth? They were to wait only a few days for the information. On the Day of Pentecost the Holy Spirit came and, through John and Peter and Jude and Paul, He unfolded the mystery, the mystery of this present waiting age between Jesus' Ascension and His coming again, between the Cross and the kingdom age. This interval has already lasted nineteen hundred years. It was a deep mystery to the disciples. It had not been revealed in the Old Testament. It was not made known until after Pentecost. Concerning this mystery of the present Church age while the kingdom is postponed and He is calling out His Bride, Paul says in Ephesians 3,

> . . . that by revelation he (God) made known unto me the mystery; . . .
>
> (Whereby, when ye read, ye may understand my knowledge in the mystery of Christ)

> Which in other ages was not made known unto the sons
> of men, as it is now revealed unto his holy apostles and
> prophets by the Spirit . . .
> Unto me, who am less than the least of all saints, is
> this grace given, that I should preach among the Gentiles
> the unsearchable riches of Christ;
> And to make all men see what is the fellowship of the
> mystery, which from the beginning of the world hath been
> hid in God, who created all things by Jesus Christ (Ephe-
> sians 3:3-5, 8-9).

This present age, then, is the age which was a mystery before Pentecost and still is a mystery to the unbeliever. There
are at least eight things peculiar to this particular Church
age and dispensation which are called mysteries in the New
Testament. They are as follows:

1. The mystery of the incarnation of Christ (I Timothy
   3:16).
2. The mystery of Israel's rejection (Romans 11:25).
3. The mystery of the Body of Christ (Ephesians 3:6).
4. The mystery of the Bride of Christ (Ephesians 5:32).
5. The mystery of the Rapture of the Church (I
   Corinthians 15:51).
6. The mystery of the ministry of the Church (Revelation 1:20).
7. The mystery of iniquity (I Thessalonians 2:7).
8. The mystery of Babylon (Revelation 17:5).

All these mysteries mentioned in the New Testament belong
to this present age. In I Corinthians 15 Paul introduces us to
the mystery of the Rapture, at the Lord Jesus' coming, which
we are studying in these chapters.

THE ORDER OF EVENTS

When Jesus comes, a number of dramatic, swiftly-moving
events will follow with lightning-like rapidity. First, the dead
in Christ shall be raised at the shout of our Lord. Soon after,
in a moment, all living believers will be suddenly changed into

their glorified deathless, sinless, eternal bodies. Then, together, these will rise to meet the Lord in the air. Here is Paul's description of this event in I Corinthians 15:52 once again. He says, "for the trumpet shall sound, and the dead shall be raised incorruptible, and we shall be changed."

The dead in Christ are raised first. Then, the living believers will be changed. Now all of this occurs in the twinkling of an eye, at the last trump. This trump is the last trump for the Church. After this last trump at the Rapture of the Church, there will follow, of course, other trumpets—seven of them in Revelation during the Tribulation alone. These subsequent trumpets, however, have no relation to the raptured saints. The trumpets in the Tribulation as described in Revelation only announce the doom of the unbelievers. The last trump in I Corinthians 15 is for the Church and announces her resurrection, her homegoing. It is well to remember not to confuse the last trump of the believers in I Corinthians 15 and I Thessalonians 4 with the trumpets of judgment to follow upon the Christ-rejectors later on.

At the Trump

At the sound of this trumpet the dead in Christ shall rise first. Then living believers will be changed. The order is repeated in verse 53:

> For this corruptible must put on incorruption, and this mortal must put on immortality.
>
> So when this corruptible shall have put on incorruption, and this mortal shall have put on immortality, then shall be brought to pass the saying that is written, Death is swallowed up in victory (I Corinthians 15:53-54).

Corruptible and Mortal

Two words are used by Paul to describe the bodies of the dead and the living saints at the Rapture. The first are called "corruptible," the second, "mortal." Corruptible and mortal are not the same. A corruptible body is a dead body, subject to the corruption of death. A mortal body is a living body not yet dead but subject to death. The corruptible are mentioned first, and then, after that, the mortal. This is the order which Paul uses. "For this corruptible must put on incorruption, and this mortal must put on immortality."

This, then, is the order. The corruptible dead will be raised first, and then the mortal living will be changed. In all the references to the Resurrection, at Jesus' coming, this order applies only to the saints of God. The lost are not raised at this time, but remain in their graves for at least another one thousand years. John says in Revelation 20:5, "But the rest of the dead lived not again until the thousand years were finished."

Thousands of Christians live a life of gloom and despair because they have never been taught this blessed, precious truth of the certain, personal, imminent return of the Lord Jesus to catch away His Bride before God's awful Judgment breaks upon this earth. A striking illustration is found in John 11, in the account of the death of Lazarus, the brother of Mary and Martha. Lazarus had died and his two sisters were heartbroken. Then Jesus comes, and Martha runs out to meet Him, and half-accusingly, half-despairingly, she cries out, "Lord, if thou hadst been here, my brother would not have died." It is then that Jesus assures her that there will be a resurrection, and says, "Thy brother shall live again." This was no news for Martha. She knew and believed that, but it seemed so far away, and she wanted Lazarus *now*. So she replies to our Lord, "I know that he shall rise again in the resurrection at the last day" (John 11:24).

THE LAST DAY

The last day! Ah, yes, he will arise at the last day at the end of the world, says Martha. How many there are like poor Martha who believe all the dead shall rise together at one time in a general Resurrection in the last day at the end of the world. Maybe you are one of those who believe just that. Then listen to Jesus' answer to Martha. Martha was a believer, a good, sincere post-millennialist who did not yet know the blessed truth of the first Resurrection and the pre-Tribulation, pre-millennial Rapture of the Church. Jesus comes with a new revelation which comforts Martha's heart and makes her dry her tears when He says,

> I am the resurrection, and the life: he that believeth on me, though he were dead, yet shall he live:
> And whosoever liveth and believeth in me shall never die (John 11:25-26).

Do not hurry over that passage. It is important. For that reason let us repeat it. "He that believeth on me, though he were dead, yet shall he live." Here is the Resurrection of dead believers, literally, bodily resurrected. They come first, and then, after that, "He that liveth and believeth in me shall never die."

Here, then, is the changing of the ones who will be alive when the dead in Christ rise. You will notice again that the order is the same. The dead in Christ shall rise first, and then the living believers shall be changed. That may happen any moment. "He that believeth on me, though he were dead, yet shall he live." That's Lazarus. When that event takes place, when all the saints of God shall rise, then those who live and believe shall never die. "But," said our Lord to Martha, "this need not wait until the last day or the general resurrection. Believest thou this, Martha?" She answered, "Yes, I do." Then she dried her tears, called her sister Mary and, a few moments later, saw an actual illustration of the imminent Rapture and Resurrection of the believers as Lazarus actually came to life from the tomb.

So, too, at the coming of Christ. It, too, may happen at any moment. It will not have to wait until the last day. It may be tomorrow. It might even be today. Then, the dead in Christ will be raised and we shall be changed, brought together with our loved ones. Every tear will be dried and we shall go to live in perfect peace and bliss and sinless joy with Him forever. That is our "blessed hope." In the midst of a world that is plunged in deepest gloom and darkness, with threatenings of judgment on every hand, we can look up and say,

> It may be at morn, when the day is awakening,
> When sunlight through shadows and darkness is breaking,
> That Jesus will come in the fullness of glory,
> To receive from the world "His own."
>
> It may be at mid-day; it may be at twilight;
> It may be, perchance, that the blackness of midnight
> Will burst into light in the blaze of His glory,
> When Jesus receives "His own."
>
> Oh joy! oh delight! should we go without dying,
> No sickness, no sadness, no dread and no crying,
> Caught up thro' the clouds with the Lord into glory,
> When Jesus receives "His own."
>
> O Lord Jesus, how long? how long
> E'er we shout the glad song.
> "Christ returneth!" Hallelujah! Hallelujah! Amen!
> Hallelujah! Amen.

EVEN SO, COME, LORD JESUS!

CHAPTER TWENTY-THREE

The Key of Prophecy

The Bible is a Book of mysteries, deep, dark profound mysteries. Yet, at the same time, the Bible is a glorious revelation, an open Book, easy to understand, simple to comprehend, as open as the face of a clock. These two statements are not contradictory at all, but perfectly harmonious. To the unregenerate mind the Bible is foolishness and full of inexplicable, mysterious symbols and nonsensical folly. To the born-again, enlightened believer, this same Book is the essence of logic, the brightest picture of the things which are wholly unbelievable to the unregenerate. The Bible is like a house with many rooms. A house may be full of mystery to the outsider. Yet, its contents and its interior are no secret to the one who holds the key to the lock and has access to the house. The secret code of our nation's military information is a mystifying, maddening jumble and scramble of meaningless symbols to the enemy. It is an open book to those who possess the key to the code. So it is with the Bible. To the unregenerate heart the Bible is a mysterious compilation of meaningless contradictions. The natural man cannot receive the things of the spirit of God, for they are foolishness to him. But of the same Book the believer can say, "Thy word is a lamp for my feet, and a light upon my path," and "The entrance of thy Word giveth light."

Jesus said, "Except a man be born again, he cannot see." Paul the Apostle says, "The God of this age hath blinded the eyes of them that believe not, lest the glorious light of the gospel of Christ who is the image of God should shine upon them." You must first have the key, before you can unlock the Book. The first key is "Ye must be born again." The simplest child of God, unschooled and uneducated, will know infinitely more of the Bible in its spiritual content and revelation than the most educated scholar who has never been born again by the spirit of God. That is the reason why a little child, believing in the Lord Jesus, finds things in this Book which the wise and the prudent of this world can never see. The unregenerate man reads this Book, yet misses the glowing, thrilling truths of the deity of Christ, His virgin birth, His substitutionary death, His bodily resurrection, His coming again, although they are as clear as the nose on one's face to the believer. You cannot know this Book until you know its Author.

Many Other Keys

There are many other keys to this house of revelation, the Bible. Regeneration is the key which opens the *front* door. Even the believer must learn to open the many doors which lead to the various rooms by the use of other keys which God has given. These keys are many—the key of literal interpretation, the key of rightly dividing the Word of truth, the key of first mention, the key of context, the key of prayer, the key of comparing Scripture with Scripture and many others.

An Illustration

As an illustration of this truth, here is a key which will open a room in this great Bible House which, to many Christians, has remained closed until this time. It is the key to the Second Coming room. On no subject in Scripture has there been more confusion among believers than the subject of the Second Coming and the return of the Lord Jesus Christ. There are a legion of interpretations and speculations concerning this subject. Most Christians believe that Jesus will come at the end of the world at which time He will call all men before Him in a general judgment. The sheep will be separated from the goats and the sheep go to heaven and the goats go to hell. Beyond this, many converted Christians never go, and so miss one of the most glorious, most blessed rooms of revelation in the house of the Bible.

THE BIBLE PICTURE

The key which unlocks the truth of Christ's Second Coming we shall call the "key of distinction." Unless we discover the difference, the distinction between the two phases of the Second Coming of Christ, we can never know the truth or the joy of that blessed hope of Christ's return. Let me make clear just what I mean. There are two distinct groups of passages in the Bible describing the Second Advent. One group of passages speaks of a secret Coming of the Lord Jesus to take out His Church at the Rapture. Another group of passages speaks of a public coming of Jesus *to* this earth in the judgment to set up His kingdom. The first, the coming of Christ for His Church, we call the Rapture or Translation. The second event is His coming again with His Church to reign upon the earth. Before giving you a number of passages to illustrate this, let me repeat, this is the key to the understanding of the Second Coming of Christ. Unless we learn to distinguish between His coming *in* the air, *for* His Church, *before* the Tribulation, and His coming *to* this earth, *with* His Church, *after* the tribulation, we shall never be able to understand the Bible revelation concerning the Second Coming of the Lord Jesus Christ. The whole doctrine will remain shrouded in mystery and leave us in a state of confusion and in a fog of uncertainty, until we learn the difference between the Rapture before the Tribulation and the Second Coming after the Tribulation. This is the key. Use it, and experience the thrill of your life.

The Evidence

Here are some Scriptures to illustrate just exactly what we mean. In I Thessalonians 5:2, we read, "The day of the Lord so cometh as a thief in the night." Here we have the coming of Christ described and referred to as a "thief." Paul had been speaking of the coming of Christ in the air in the portion just preceding this passage in I Thessalonians 4. He had said, "For the Lord Himself shall descend from heaven with a shout." At this time, we are told, the dead will be raised, the living believers changed and together they will be raptured or caught up, for that is the meaning of "Rapture." This, says Paul, will be like a thief. How and when does a thief come? He comes in the night, he comes when the occupants are asleep, he comes when it is dark, he leaves before the owner awakens, and he takes away only that which has value. So shall the coming of Christ be, says Paul, in the Rapture. It will be like a thief, taking only the precious things (the Church), snatching them secretly away before the rest of the world knows what has happened.

Every Eye Shall See Him

Quite another picture of the Coming of Christ is found in Revelation 1:7. "Behold, he cometh with clouds; and every eye shall see him, and they also which pierced him: and all kindreds of the earth shall wail because of him." There is a vast difference in these two events. This is a public appearing when every eye sees Him. It results in wailing and weeping. When He comes as a thief for His Bride, there is rejoicing. Paul says, "Comfort one another with these words." The secret Rapture is a time of joy; the public appearing is a time of judgment and doom for the rejectors of Christ.

In the Air

Let me give you another example. In I Thessalonians 4 we read, "For the Lord Himself shall descend from heaven with a shout." At this time He does not come to this earth at all, but stops in mid air. We (the raised dead and the changed believers) rise to meet Him *in the air.* This is the Rapture.

In Zechariah 14, verse 4, describing the Second Coming of the Lord, the prophet says, "And his feet shall stand in that day upon the mount of Olives, which is before Jerusalem on the east . . . "

In verse 9 of the same chapter he tells us: "And the Lord shall be king over all the earth: in that day shall there be one Lord, and his name one" (Zechariah 14:9).

You may have noticed that in the first passage in Thessalonians, He comes in the air, and we meet Him there. In the second Scripture He comes to this earth. His feet will stand upon the Mount of Olives and we shall be with Him. The first event, the "Secret event," is the Translation of the Church; the second event is His public revelation when He comes to this earth.

In passing, let me remind you that in every case where the Rapture is mentioned, it is given as a comfort and a "blessed hope" to the believer. In every passage dealing with His coming to the earth publicly, it is in judgment and accompanied with solemn warnings and dire promises of judgment.

In II Thessalonians 2:1 Paul mentions both these phases of the Coming of Christ. He says, "Now we beseech you, brethren, by the coming of our Lord Jesus Christ, *and* by our gathering together unto him . . ."

Notice here that Paul mentions:

1. The coming of Jesus Christ
2. Our gathering together unto Him

To say both refer to the same thing is to accuse God of needless repetition and ambiguity. They are two separate events.

In Titus 2:13, Paul says, "Looking for that blessed hope, *and* the glorious appearing of our great God and our Saviour

Jesus Christ!" Here again are two statements describing the *two* phases:

1. That blessed hope—the Rapture of the Church
2. The glorious appearing of our Lord Jesus Christ—His public coming to this earth

Two Openings In Heaven

Scores of other passages might be quoted, but we take time for just one more, namely, the two openings in heaven referred to in the Book of the Revelation. Just a word first about the outline of this great closing book of the Bible. You will recall that the first three chapters of Revelation give us the history of the Church, prewritten by the apostle John, from Pentecost to the coming of Christ. The Church is mentioned fourteen times in these three chapters, the first three chapters of Revelation. It records the present Church age under the figure of seven churches from Ephesus to Laodicea. Then, in Revelation 4:1, the Church is caught away. John, caught up into heaven, describes it in these words, "After this I looked, and, behold, a door was opened in heaven: and the first voice which I heard was as it were of a trumpet talking with me; which said, Come up hither . . ." (Revelation 4:1).

The language indicates that this is the Rapture, with the voice, and the trumpet and the call to come up, all identifying it as that event. John, representing the Church, is immediately caught away into heaven. From here on the Church is never again seen. She never appears in the rest of Revelation until she comes with Christ as the Bride in Revelation chapter 19. The chapters following Revelation 4 record the Tribulation upon this earth. We find the 144,000 of Israel dealt with and God judging the nations. Search as you will, however, you cannot find any reference to the Church after the fourth chapter of Revelation. Though mentioned fourteen times in the first three chapters, the Church is entirely absent after that, for Revelation 5 to 19 deals with the Tribulation on the earth. The Church is not seen; she is not here. She is with her Lord in heaven, caught up in Revelation 4, before the Tribulation period.

THE SECOND OPENING

The second time heaven opens is in Revelation 19:11. The Tribulation, described under the seven seals, the seven trumpets, the seven vials, is over, and now we read, "And I saw heaven opened, and behold a white horse; and he that sat upon him was called Faithful and True, and in righteousness he doth judge and make war" (Revelation 19:11). This is the second and the final opening of heaven. The first was in Revelation 4. There, *John goes up*. Here, in Rev. 19:11, *Jesus comes down* to earth to judge the world. I trust that you will see the difference. The first is secret and filled with comfort. The second opening is public and fraught with judgment and doom.

When Jesus comes after the Tribulation, the saints will come with Him, for John says, "And the armies which were in heaven followed him upon white horses, clothed in fine linen, white and clean" (Revelation 19:14).

Here, then, the redeemed are caught up secretly at the first opening in heaven in Revelation 4:1. In Revelation 19:11, they are coming back with Him publicly.

This is the order: first, the Rapture; then, the Tribulation, then, the Second Coming, and, then, His glorious, millennial reign. This is the key. Until you learn to use it, the Book defies intelligent opening. Learn this key, and come out of the fog.

A closing thought. You will meet this Jesus some day, either in the Rapture or in the Judgment. Will you not make your decision right now? Jesus Christ is coming again. It is surer than death itself. The very last promise in the Bible is this,

"He which testifieth these things saith, Surely I come quickly. Amen" (Revelation 22:20).

Are you ready? One of these days it will all be over. Your eternal destiny will depend on what you do with Him *now*.

Trust Him now who said, "Come unto me, all ye that labor and are heavy laden, and I will give you rest" (Matthew 11: 28).

CHAPTER TWENTY-FOUR

The Translation of the Church

But I would not have you to be ignorant, brethren, concerning them which are asleep, that ye sorrow not, even as others which have no hope.

For if we believe that Jesus died and rose again, even so them also which sleep in Jesus will God bring with him.

For this we say unto you by the word of the Lord, that we which are alive and remain unto the coming of the Lord shall not prevent them which are asleep.

For the Lord himself shall descend from heaven with a shout, with the voice of the archangel, and with the trump of God: and the dead in Christ shall rise first:

Then we which are alive and remain shall be caught up together with them in the clouds, to meet the Lord in the air: and so shall we ever be with the Lord.

Wherefore comfort ye one another with these words (I Thessalonians 4:13-18).

This is a funeral sermon. Paul the Apostle, under inspiration, tells us that this passage should be used at the funerals of all believers. In the closing verse he says, "Wherefore comfort ye one another with these words." This is in the form of a command. The occasion for these words was the death of some of the Thessalonian Christians. Their loved ones were sad at heart, depressed and confused. Paul gives them, in this first epistle to the Thessalonian Church, the only hope and comfort for sorrowing, bereaved believers in every age.

THE OCCASION

The occasion for the writing of the Epistle to the Thessalonians is quite evident. On Paul's second missionary journey he had stopped at Thessalonica for about two weeks. During his stay he had preached the Gospel in all its fullness. As a result, a company of these Thessalonians, who had been saved and soundly converted, had assembled together into a local church, the church of Thessalonica. Paul had not only preached the Gospel of salvation, the death and burial and Resurrection of the Lord Jesus, but had also preached to them something about the Second Coming, the imminent return of Jesus, to set up His Kingdom. Evidently the Christians in Thessalonica believed in the imminent return of the Lord Jesus Christ. They were constantly waiting for His return, expecting at His coming to enter into the glorious kingdom with Him. Then, something happened which greatly disturbed them, for, while they were waiting for Jesus to come, some of these believers died, or as the text says, "fell asleep." This confused them greatly, for they had been led to believe that they would live until the coming of Christ. This was the impression they had gained from Paul's preaching. Naturally, since Paul had spent only about two weeks among them, his teaching on this great theme of Christ's return was rather fragmentary and lacking in many of the details. There were as yet none of the books of the New Testament written to which they could refer, so they were limited in their knowledge of this truth to that which Paul had revealed to them during his brief stay among them. They knew Paul had taught them that when Jesus came, then *all* would share in the kingdom glory. Now, when some had died, they wondered about these and their place in the kingdom. You see, these Christians in Thessalonica as yet knew nothing of the first resurrection of the saints before the millennial kingdom. That truth was only fully revealed in the books of the New Testament, especially Paul's writings, none of which were as yet in existence. They, therefore, feared that when Jesus came, they (who were alive) would go into the kingdom with Him, and that these departed loved ones would not share in the millennial reign of Christ on earth. They still believed in a general resurrection at the end of the age and the end of time, and the end of the world. They were post-millennial and believed in a post-millennial resurrection. No wonder, therefore, that they were confused. No wonder they were sorrowing. No wonder they were in doubt.

PAUL'S ANSWER

Paul hears about their confusion and distress. He immediately sits down to write this earliest of all his epistles in order to set their hearts at rest. He says, "But I would not have you to be ignorant, brethren, concerning them which are asleep, that ye sorrow not, even as others which have no hope" (I Thessalonians 4:13).

This, then, was the occasion for his writing. They were sorrowing over those that were asleep. Paul does not want them to experience undue and unnecessary sorrow because of their ignorance of God's plan. That is why he gives this glorious, marvelous revelation called by him in Titus, "that blessed hope."

First, Paul reminds them in the fourteenth verse, that, if they believe that Jesus died and rose again, then the Lord Jesus Himself will also bring their loved ones with Him when He returns. That is the message of the Gospel, that is the one condition on which this comfort may be appropriated. We must be believers in the Lord Jesus Christ, or there is no comfort for us in the hour of death. Then, in the next verse, verse fifteen, he assures them that there is no doubt about this at all, and continues, "For this we say unto you by the word of the Lord, that we which are alive and remain unto the coming of the Lord shall not prevent them which are asleep" (I Thessalonians 4:15).

The word translated "prevent" here is much better rendered "precede." It is *phthana* in the original Greek and means "to go beforehand." What Paul says, therefore, is this, "Don't worry anymore about your departed loved ones not sharing in the glory of His kingdom, for we which are alive and remain unto the coming of the Lord shall not precede, we shall not go on before those which are asleep in the Lord Jesus."

THE ORDER OF EVENTS

Then, having stated the fact of this great event, he goes on to give the details. We repeat it again, for, though it is so simple a child can understand, thousands have missed it.

> For the Lord himself shall descend from heaven with a shout, with the voice of the archangel, and with the trump of God: and the dead in Christ shall rise first:
>
> Then we which are alive and remain shall be caught up together with them in the clouds, to meet the Lord in the air: and so shall we ever be with the Lord (I Thessalonians 4:16-17).

We almost feel as though we ought to offer an apology for even trying to add any kind of an explanation or exposition of this wonderful passage. It is so direct, so clear, so concise and so simple, that a child can easily understand it. Yet it is new and unknown to thousands of believers. Hundreds write to us saying, "We never hear about it in our circles. In order to get the truth of this glorious event we must get it somewhere else." Here are the simple steps in this coming wonderful meeting of the saints in the air. We outline the steps as follows.

STEP NUMBER ONE

The first thing which will happen when the rapture takes place is the descent of the Lord Jesus Christ from heaven. Paul says, "The Lord himself shall descend from heaven." It is none other than the Lord Jesus Himself. For over nineteen hundred years He has been in heaven, seated on the right hand of God, preparing a place for us and waiting for the last member of His body to be added to the Church. Then He will rise and step down from heaven, just as He went up, nineteen hundred years ago. As He approaches the earth, He stops in mid air. Please notice this carefully. In this event in I Thessalonians Jesus does *not* come all the way down to earth, but stops in the middle of the air, where He waits for us to rise and meet Him. It is very important that we recognize this fact so that we do not confuse the Rapture with His coming to the earth at a later date.

STEP NUMBER TWO

As He comes down from heaven into the air He shouts, the archangel speaks and the trumpet is blown. He comes, says Paul, with a shout, with the voice of the archangel, and with the trump of God. The voice or the shout is the call to the waiting Church here below. At this shout of the Lord the saints who sleep will arise from the dead (that is, their bodies), and living believers will be instantaneously changed into glorified beings. The shout, therefore, is specifically for the Church of the Lord Jesus. Then we notice that the archangel also speaks. The archangel in Scripture is Michael, God's protector of the nation of Israel. In every single instance where the archangel Michael is mentioned in the Scriptures, he is presented to us in the role of the defender of the nation of Israel against all of her persecutors. After the Church is gone Israel's greatest persecution will begin, called the "time of Jacob's trouble." The Lord, therefore, sends Michael, the archangel, at this same time to assure the faithful remnant of Israel that they will be delivered through this Tribulation. The third thing is the trumpet, the trumpet which calls the Church to rise and meet her Lord. Also, incidentally, this trump of judgment announces the doom of the wicked in the Tribulation period.

STEP NUMBER THREE

At this shout of the Lord the saints will rise. Paul says, "And the dead in Christ shall arise first." All who have died in the faith, from Adam till that moment, will come out of their graves. Immediately after, in the twinkling of an eye, those of us alive when this happens will be changed in a moment from mortal to immortal. Our bodies will be sinlessly, deathlessly, glorified in an instant, in a moment of time. Our redemption of spirit, soul and body will then, for the first time, be fully complete.

STEP NUMBER FOUR

The next thing is the reunion of the raised, resurrected saints with the changed and living believers. Even before we meet our Lord Jesus Christ we will meet our departed loved ones again. Our Lord is so considerate of the tender, human ties which were broken when our loved ones left us, He is so sympathetic with our sorrow at being bereaved, He is so considerate of the burning desire we have to see our departed loved ones again, that He will permit us, in His love and grace, to meet them first, and to greet them, to be reunited with them first, even before we meet our Lord. Much as He longs to have us meet Him in the air, He will first take into consideration our broken, human ties. He is willing to wait Himself, until we meet them first. Then, together, we meet Him in the air. Many have missed this tender revelation in the passage, but here it is again: "Then we which are alive and remain shall be caught up *together with them* in the clouds, to meet the Lord in the air."

Are you sure that you caught the implication of that wonderful phrase? Don't miss it. We shall be caught up *together-together with them*. First, we are brought together. Then, we rise to meet the Lord *together*. How wonderful! My sister and I, the only two alive of our family, will meet our precious mother and father, our brothers and our sister. Then, as a complete family, we shall rise to meet our Lord in the air.

STEP NUMBER FIVE

The next event will be our meeting with *Him*. See *Him*. *Him*—the Man who died for us and gave Himself upon the Cross of Calvary. Then, we shall be forever with the Lord. In the light of this it is no wonder that Paul concludes this wonderful passage with these words, "Wherefore comfort ye one another with these words."

Surely the world holds no comfort as we stand by the grave by our departed loved ones, realizing that these bodies must be committed to the ground until that day of resurrection. Only as we can look beyond the empty grave into the open heavens from whence the Lord Jesus Christ will come to bring the spirits of these departed ones with Him, and then raise these corruptible bodies into incorruption, can we find any comfort which causes a bit of light to shine through the darkness of our sorrow and our tears. This has been the hope of every true believer in every age. It becomes more and more so in this age in which we are now living. Paul tells us in Philippians,

> For our conversation is in heaven; from whence also we look for the Saviour, the Lord Jesus Christ:
> Who shall change our vile body, that it may be fashioned like unto his glorious body, according to the working whereby he is able even to subdue all things unto himself (Philippians 3:20-21).

> He which testifieth these things, saith; Surely I come quickly. Amen (Revelation 22:20).

The M. R. De Haan Classic Library

M. R. De Haan spoke to millions of listeners each week for some twenty-seven years on the *Radio Bible Class* broadcast. His academic training included a degree from Hope College, a medical degree from the University of Illinois Medical College, and further study at Western Theological Seminary. He was the author of more than twenty books and countless daily devotionals in *Our Daily Bread*, published by RBC Ministries of Grand Rapids, Michigan.

Anyone interested in solid biblical studies for personal growth will find these titles to be rich sources of insight and inspiration.

Adventures in Faith: Studies in the Life of Abraham
ISBN 0-8254-2481-x   192 pp.   paperback

Daniel the Prophet
ISBN 0-8254-2475-5   344 pp.   paperback

Pentecost and After: Studies in the Book of Acts
ISBN 0-8254-2482-8   184 pp.   paperback

Portraits of Christ in Genesis
ISBN 0-8254-2476-3   192 pp.   paperback

The Romance of Redemption: Studies in the Book of Ruth
ISBN 0-8254-2480-1   184 pp.   paperback

The Second Coming of Jesus
ISBN 0-8254-2483-6   176 pp.   paperback

The Signs of the Times
ISBN 0-8254-2484-4   184 pp.   paperback

Studies in First Corinthians
ISBN 0-8254-2478-x   192 pp.   paperback

Studies in Galatians
ISBN 0-8254-2477-1   192 pp.   paperback

Studies in Hebrews
ISBN 0-8254-2479-8   216 pp.   paperback

Available from Christian bookstores or

kregel
PUBLICATIONS

P.O. Box 2607 • Grand Rapids, MI 49501-2607